The British Army of Queen Victoria, 1837–1901

Gabriele Esposito is a military historian who works as a freelance author and researcher for some of the most important publishing houses in the military history sector. In particular, he is an expert specializing in uniformology: his interests and expertise range from the ancient civilizations to modern post-colonial conflicts. During recent years, he has conducted and published several researches on the military history of the Latin American countries, with special attention on the War of the Triple Alliance and the War of the Pacific. He is among the leading experts on the military history of the Italian Wars of Unification and the Spanish Carlist Wars. His books and essays are published on a regular basis by Osprey Publishing, Pen & Sword, Winged Hussar Publishing and Libreria Editrice Goriziana; he is also the author of numerous military history articles, appearing in specialized magazines like *Ancient Warfare Magazine*, *Medieval Warfare Magazine*, *The Armourer*, *History of War*, *Guerres et Histoire*, *Focus Storia* and *Focus Storia Wars*.

The British Army of Queen Victoria, 1837–1901

Organization, Uniforms and Equipment

Gabriele Esposito

Pen & Sword
MILITARY

First published in Great Britain in 2025 by
Pen & Sword Military
An imprint of
Pen & Sword Books Limited
Yorkshire – Philadelphia

Copyright © Pen & Sword Books Limited 2025

ISBN 978 1 03610 329 3

The right of Gabriele Esposito to be identified as
Author of this Work has been asserted by him in accordance
with the Copyright, Designs and Patents Act 1988.

A CIP catalogue record for this book is
available from the British Library

All rights reserved. No part of this book may be reproduced, transmitted, downloaded, decompiled or reverse engineered in any form or by any means, electronic or mechanical including photocopying, recording or by any information storage and retrieval system, without permission from the Publisher in writing. No part of this book may be used or reproduced in any manner for the purpose of training artificial intelligence technologies or systems.

Typeset by Mac Style
Printed and bound in India by Replika Press Pvt. Ltd.

The Publisher's authorised representative in the EU for product safety is
Authorised Rep Compliance Ltd., Ground Floor, 71 Lower Baggot Street,
Dublin D02 P593, Ireland.
www.arccompliance.com

For a complete list of Pen & Sword titles please contact:

PEN & SWORD BOOKS LIMITED
47 Church Street, Barnsley, South Yorkshire, S70 2AS, England
E-mail: enquiries@pen-and-sword.co.uk
Website: www.pen-and-sword.co.uk
or
PEN AND SWORD BOOKS
1950 Lawrence Road, Havertown, PA 19083, USA
E-mail: uspen-and-sword@casematepublishers.com
Website: www.penandswordbooks.com

Contents

Acknowledgements vi
Introduction vii

Chapter 1 Guard and Line Infantry 1

Chapter 2 Rifles and Light Infantry 48

Chapter 3 Guard and Heavy Cavalry 67

Chapter 4 Light Cavalry 98

Chapter 5 Artillery and Technical Corps 127

Chapter 6 Royal Marines 155

Chapter 7 Volunteer Legions and Foreign Units 163

Chapter 8 The Crimean War, 1853–1856 174

Chapter 9 The Indian Campaigns of the British Army 179

Chapter 10 The Asian Campaigns of the British Army 195

Chapter 11 The African Campaigns of the British Army 198

Chapter 12 The American Campaigns of the British Army 221

Chapter 13 The British Army in Australia and New Zealand 225

Bibliography 228
Index 229

Acknowledgements

This book is dedicated to my magnificent parents, Maria Rosaria and Benedetto, for the immense love and fundamental support that they always give me. Thanks to their precious advice, deriving from long experience, the present book is much better than I could have ever envisioned. A very special thanks goes to Philip Sidnell, the commissioning editor of my books for Pen & Sword: his love for history and passion for publishing are the key factors behind the success of our publications. Many thanks also to the production manager of this title, Matt Jones, for his excellent work and great enthusiasm. A special mention is due to Tony Walton, for the magnificent work of editing that he makes for all my books.

Introduction

When Queen Victoria ascended to the throne of Great Britain in 1837, the British Empire was experiencing an age of great splendour and expansion that continued for several decades. Britain emerged from the Napoleonic Wars in 1815 as the world's leading colonial power, controlling extensive territories in every corner of the globe: from India and Canada to South Africa and Australia, to name just a few. During the long reign of Queen Victoria, which ended in 1901, Britain consolidated its position as the world's greatest naval and commercial power by conducting a series of victorious military campaigns in its colonies. Such wars, which were often fought very far from Europe, involved the British Army as their main protagonist. After their triumph at the Battle of Waterloo in 1815, British forces underwent a major process of reorganization and modernization that lasted until the 1880s. They started to be organized on a much more professional footing than before and began to be strongly linked with the home communities from which their units were recruited. In this book we will follow the evolution of the British Army throughout the reign of Queen Victoria, from the demobilization that took place after the end of the Napoleonic Wars to the expansion that characterized the closing decades of the nineteenth century. We will describe all the major organizational reforms that affected Britain's military forces, analysing in detail the internal composition of the various branches of service. The core of the British Army during this whole period comprised the regiments of foot of the line infantry. These, wearing their iconic scarlet red tunics, defended and expanded the boundaries of the British Empire by fighting against a huge variety of enemies. The foot units of the British Army, however, did not consist only of line infantry; there were also several regiments defined as 'light infantry' as well as two elite corps equipped with rifled weapons since their creation (the King's Royal Rifle Corps and the Rifle Brigade). The line infantry also included the famous Highland regiments, which had a series of peculiarities that made them different from any other troop type. The British Army of Queen Victoria deployed a sizeable cavalry contingent too, which underwent significant tactical reforms during the post-Waterloo period. After the Napoleonic Wars, new kinds of mounted units were introduced and the British cavalry came to comprise five troop types by the beginning of the Crimean

War in 1853: dragoon guards, dragoons, light dragoons, hussars and lancers. Each of these had their own peculiar tactical features and uniforms. Both the infantry and cavalry of the British Army included various elite units having 'Guard' status, which in many respects were very different from the rest of Britain's armed forces: the Grenadiers Guards, Coldstream Guards, Scots Guards, Life Guards and Horse Guards. The infantry and cavalry were supported by the technical corps, the quality of which were extremely high since they were manned according to rigid principles based on meritocracy. The most important technical corps was the Royal Artillery, which included a very effective mounted branch. During the nineteenth century, British artillery became increasingly professional and started to include several different kinds of units. The other technical corps of the British Army included the Royal Engineers – who played a fundamental role in all the campaigns that took place during the reign of Queen Victoria – as well as the Royal Army Service Corps, which performed important logistic functions. The book will also cover the contingents of naval infantry and naval artillery, i.e. the Royal Marines and the Royal Marine Artillery; the latter, despite being part of the British navy and not of the British Army, participated alongside the land forces in all the wars that were fought by Britain. There were also various legions made up of British volunteers who fought abroad during the first half of the nineteenth century, as well as foreign military units in British service. The former – which were deployed in South America, Portugal and Spain (some admittedly just prior to Victoria's accession to the throne, but which I have nevertheless decided to include in this volume as representative of where British troops served in the mid-nineteenth century) – represented a little-known tool of British foreign policy, while the latter, raised during the Crimean War, were recruited from several different countries. For all the categories of military units listed above, this volume will provide extensive details on their history and organization, as well as their uniforms and weapons. The nineteenth century was an age of great change for both military dress (several different uniform regulations were introduced) and equipment (flintlock smoothbore muskets were replaced with percussion rifles, which were in turn substituted by breech-loading weapons). The various chapters of the book are illustrated with many colour pictures, which aim to give the reader a clear idea of how the British Army looked like during one of the most splendid ages in the history of military uniforms.

Chapter 1

Guard and Line Infantry

History and Organization

All the European armies of the early nineteenth century comprised a certain number of 'Guard' units, which made up an elite within the military forces of each country. These could be small bodyguard corps, with a main function of escorting the monarchs, or larger combatant units with superior training and morale. In Great Britain, the Royal Guards had a very long tradition and consisted of combatant units having a special status and performing peculiar duties. Their infantry component consisted of three regiments: 1st Foot Guards, or Grenadier Guards; 2nd Foot Guards, or Coldstream Guards; and 3rd Foot Guards, or Scots Guards. Each of these units had a unique history, from which their nicknames came. The 1st Foot Guards were created in 1665, by merging together two infantry regiments that already had 'Guard' status and duties: Lord Wentworth's Regiment and John Russell's Regiment. The first of these had been raised in 1656 by the future Charles II during his exile in the Spanish Netherlands (present-day Belgium); it initially consisted of professional soldiers who had followed the future monarch in his exile and were loyal to the Stuarts. With the Restoration in 1660, the unit returned to England and became part of the reorganized English army. John Russell's Regiment was created in 1660, after Charles II came back to England; it mirrored the functions and structure of Lord Wentworth's Regiment and soon became a duplicate of it. In 1665, it was decided to unite the two guard regiments into a single unit, which received the new denomination of the 1st Regiment of Foot Guards. The unified corps adopted its nickname of Grenadier Guards only in 1815, following a Royal Proclamation that transformed the regiment into a grenadier unit. From the late seventeenth century, grenadier units enjoyed a superior status, the name being restricted to heavy infantry corps having special training and equipment. During the Napoleonic Wars, the French grenadiers of Napoleon's Imperial Guard became the most famous heavy infantrymen in the world due to their courage and discipline on the battlefield. When they were defeated at Waterloo by Wellington's 1st Foot Guards, the British unit was awarded the new denomination of Grenadier Guards, a name it retains to this day.

2   The British Army of Queen Victoria, 1837–1901

Officer of the Foot Guards in 1815, wearing the newly adopted bearskin. (*ASKB*)

Officer of the Coldstream Guards in the 1820s, wearing a Regency shako.

Guard and Line Infantry

Grenadier of the Coldstream Guards in 1822, with the newly introduced cuff flaps.

The 2nd Foot Guards were created in 1650, as one of the infantry regiments that made up Cromwell's New Model Army. Initially known as Monck's Regiment of Foot, in 1660 it backed the Restoration of the Stuarts and made an epic march of five weeks from Coldstream (in Berwickshire) to London in order to support Charles II. Due to this episode, it soon received the nickname of Coldstream Guards from the name of the village where the elite infantrymen had started their march. After the Restoration, the regiment remained in London to keep order in the capital. In 1661, thanks to its loyalty to the king, it received the new official denomination of The Lord General's Regiment of Foot Guards. Although the 2nd Foot Guards was older than the 1st Foot Guards, it was placed as the second senior regiment of the Household Troops because it had entered royal service after the Grenadier Guards (until 1661, it had formally been part of the New Model Army and not of the royalist forces). To underline the fact that their corps was older than the 1st Foot Guards, members of the Coldstream Guards adopted as their regimental motto the phrase *'Nulli Secundus'* (i.e., 'Second to None'). In 1670, the unit adopted its definitive name of the Coldstream Regiment of Foot Guards. The 3rd Foot Guards was the oldest of the three guard regiments, but it was the last to enter English royal service; as a result, it was placed as the third senior unit of the Household Troops. The regiment was created in 1642, as part of the Scottish army rather than the English one – it should be remembered that until 1707, the Scottish military remained independent from their English equivalent as England and Scotland were two autonomous kingdoms.

Charles I, as King of Scotland, ordered the formation of what was to become the 3rd Foot Guards in order to face the Irish Rebellion of 1641. The unit was raised by the Marquess of Argyll, Archibald Campbell, and thus had as its first denomination the Marquis of Argyll's Royal Regiment. In 1650, when Charles II became King of Scotland following the execution of his father, it became a guard unit and adopted the new title of the Lyfe Guard of Foot. In 1651, following Cromwell's victories over the supporters of Charles II, the Scottish Guards were disbanded, but were re-formed ten years later when Charles II was restored to the English and Scottish thrones. Now known as the Scottish Regiment of Foot Guards, it was transferred to the establishment of the English army in 1686 and became part of the English Royal Guard. In 1712, after England and Scotland had been united into a single state in 1707, the Scots Guards were given their final denomination of the 3rd Regiment of Foot Guards.

The backbone of the three Guard regiments was represented by the NCOs, professionals who were able to skilfully train their men. It was their duty to transform young recruits into battle-hardened veterans, thereby preserving the traditions of the regiment. Obedience, endurance, loyalty and pride were the key elements behind the elite status of the foot guardsmen. Most of the common soldiers serving in the Foot Guard regiments came from the militia and thus already had some experience of military life. Under the guidance of their NCOs, they rapidly turned into professionals who were able to deal with any combat situation. Even more important than the NCOs were the officers, who gave the Foot Guard regiments their real and distinctive character. Most of the officers came from important aristocratic families of land-owners, which had long military traditions. They were known as 'Gentlemen's Sons', while the Duke of Wellington called them 'fellows in silk stockings'. However, despite such nicknames, they showed on many occasions that they were not lacking in courage. Buying an officer's commission in the guard infantry regiments was extremely costly, meaning that only the young sons of the aristocracy or of the upper middle class could do this. Daily life, in times of peace, was very expensive for such officers: it was spent in the most prestigious gentlemen's clubs of London and obliged the 'fellows in silk stockings' to invest large sums of money in order to have the most elegant uniforms and be part of high society.

By 1815, the three regiments of Foot Guards had two or three battalions each; a single battalion comprised eight field companies and two depot companies plus a small staff. Of the field companies, two had elite status and were known as flank companies since they were deployed on the flanks of the others during combat: the grenadier company (heavy infantry) and the light infantry company. The Grenadier Guards had an extra-large establishment with three battalions from 1760, while the

Guard and Line Infantry 5

NCO of the Coldstream Guards in 1822, wearing the green plume that was distinctive of light companies.

other two units of the Foot Guards had two battalions each, the same as most of the British Army's line infantry regiments. A 3rd Battalion was added to the Scots Guards in 1889, while the 3rd Battalion of the Coldstream Guards was raised during 1897. During the period 1815–54, the three regiments of the guard infantry did not see service overseas, but when Britain entered the Crimean War, it was decided to form a temporary Brigade of the Guard for service against Russia. The latter, which was disbanded at the end of hostilities, consisted of the following units: the 3rd Battalion of the Grenadier Guards, 1st Battalion of the Coldstream Guards and 1st Battalion of the Scots Guards. The brigade, being formed from veteran soldiers with extensive experience, performed extremely well during the conflict and distinguished itself at the battles of the Alma (1854), Inkerman (1854) and Sevastopol (1855). After the Crimean War, the regiments of Foot Guards sent their battalions overseas on several more occasions, always confirming their excellent military reputation. The battalions of the Grenadier Guards participated in the following campaigns: Egypt (1882), Sudan (1885 and 1898), Fourth Anglo-Ashanti War (1895) and Second Boer War (1899–1902). The Coldstream Guards and Scots Guards, meanwhile, fought in Egypt

Musician of the Coldstream Guards in 1822. Note the profusion of decorative lace that was typical of the musicians' uniforms and the green plume of light companies.

(1882) and Sudan (1885), as well as during the Second Boer War. On 1 April 1900, Queen Victoria, in order to commemorate the many Irishmen who had fought courageously during the early phase of the Second Boer War, decided to form a new regiment of Irish Guards within her Guard infantry. The new unit was created by transferring 200 Irishmen from the Grenadier Guards and choosing selected members of the line infantry regiments that were recruited in Ireland. The Irish Guards completed their organization in 1902 after Queen Victoria was succeeded by King Edward VII.

With the general demobilization that followed the end of the Napoleonic Wars, the line infantry of the British Army was restructured on ninety-one regiments. Most of these had a standard establishment of two battalions, but some regiments deployed only a single battalion and several others (among the lowest-numbered and therefore senior line infantry regiments) mustered three battalions each. Each line infantry battalion consisted of eight field companies and two depot companies, plus a small staff. Of the field companies, two were the elite flank companies of grenadiers and light infantrymen, although following the end of the Napoleonic Wars, the tactical peculiarities of the flank companies progressively disappeared since all the line infantry companies started to perform in exactly the same way. Flank companies were officially abolished and transformed into ordinary ones during 1858. Each regiment of foot was numbered but also had a specific denomination, which usually derived from the surname of the colonel who had created it or the name of the county where the unit was raised. During 1823 and 1824, six new regiments of line infantry (numbered 93–99, with the King's Royal Rifle Corps included in the line infantry's numbering) were formed. Consequently, by the outbreak of the Crimean War, the British Army could deploy a total of ninety-eight regiments of foot, some of which, despite having exactly the same features as the other line corps, bore the peculiar denomination of Fusiliers. During the seventeenth century, Fusiliers were infantry soldiers tasked with escorting the artillery train of the army, but over time they became standard line infantrymen. As a result, by the nineteenth century, the term Fusiliers no longer had any tactical meaning, being a purely honorific title. The three oldest regiments of Fusiliers existing in the British Army were the Royal Fusiliers (created in 1685), Royal Scots Fusiliers (created in 1678) and Royal Welch Fusiliers (created in 1689). As we will see in the next chapter, some of the regiments of foot were designated as light infantry, but this did not have significant practical consequences since the only 'true' light corps of the British foot troops were the two units of Rifles. The outbreak of the Indian Mutiny in 1857 had important consequences for the structure of the British line infantry, which had not been expanded during the Crimean War. In 1858, as news of the massacres of British civilians in India reached

Officer of a light infantry regiment, wearing a Regency shako and a tail-coat with coloured frontal plastron. All companies of the light infantry regiments had shoulder wings.

Line infantryman in the 1820s. Except for the Regency shako, the overall appearance is more or less the same as the pre-1815 period.

the other parts of the British Empire, the colonial authorities of Canada decided to raise a new regiment of foot for service in the Indian Subcontinent. The new unit, known as the 100th Royal Canadian Regiment of Foot, was formed from volunteers (many of whom were members of the Canadian 'Active Militia'). The regiment sailed to England and became part of the British Army as planned, but its recruiting operations in North America soon came to an end and the unit lost its Canadian identity in all but name.

Until the outbreak of the Indian Mutiny, the vast British territorial possessions in India were not ruled by the British government but by the East India Company. The company had structured its domains as three autonomous presidencies (Madras, Bengal and Bombay), each of which had its own military forces that comprised both European units and locally raised corps. The units made up of Indian soldiers, or sepoys, were the main protagonists of the bloody Indian Mutiny, with many of them rebelling against the East India Company. As a result, the European corps of the three Indian presidencies had to fight against their former comrades in order to protect British interests in India. By 1857, the company had the following European infantry regiments under its orders: the Royal Bengal Fusiliers, Bengal Fusiliers, Bengal Infantry, Royal Madras Fusiliers, Madras Light

Officer of a Highland regiment in 1825, wearing a tail-coat with coloured frontal plastron.

Infantry, Madras Infantry, Royal Bombay Fusiliers, Bombay Light Infantry and Bombay Infantry. Despite bearing different titles like 'Fusiliers' or 'Light Infantry', all these units were standard corps of line infantry, having the same basic features as those of the British Army. Despite being defined as regiments, however, they all had an internal establishment consisting of only a single battalion. The European soldiers recruited by the East India Company in Britain were not of the same quality as those who served in the regular British Army, which offered better conditions of service to potential recruits and thus the best elements wishing to serve in the military usually entered the ranks of the regulars. Most of the British soldiers serving under the flags of the East India Company were individuals who had decided to leave their homeland in search of opportunity or who lived on the margins of their home society. Some of them had experienced problems with justice, while others had no choice but to enlist as soldiers of fortune in order to earn a living. Members of the Company's European units also comprised significant numbers of whites who were recruited in India from European adventurers or mercenaries who were in search of employment. French, Swiss, German and Dutch recruits were the most commonly found, but there were also individuals of mixed ethnicity (half-European and half-Indian). Discipline and training of these soldiers were not the same as their equivalents serving in the British Army, but on most occasions they proved to be reliable fighters. A good number of them had a clear idea of what military discipline was, since it was not uncommon for a soldier from the regular army to decide to remain in India after a period of service there and enter the ranks of the military forces of the East India Company. Life in India was cheaper than in Britain, and the risks faced while serving under the flags of the East India Company were not comparable to those experienced in the regular army. The nine European infantry regiments of the East India Company played a very important rule during the suppression of the Indian Mutiny. As a result, when India was officially annexed to the dominions of the British Empire following the end of the uprising and the dissolution of the East India Company, they were not disbanded but became part of the British Army's line infantry. The Royal Bengal Fusiliers became the 101st Regiment of Foot, the Royal Madras Fusiliers was renamed the 102nd Regiment of Foot, the Royal Bombay Fusiliers became the 103rd Regiment of Foot, the Bengal Fusiliers served as the 104th Regiment of Foot, the Madras Light Infantry became the 105th Regiment of Foot, the Bombay Light Infantry became the 106th Regiment of Foot, the Bengal Infantry was transformed into the 107th Regiment of Foot, the Madras Infantry became the 108th Regiment of Foot and the Bombay Infantry was renamed the 109th Regiment of Foot.

Guard and Line Infantry 11

Private of a Highland regiment in 1825, wearing a feather bonnet. After 1822, all companies of the Highland regiments had shoulder wings.

By 1861, as a result of the organizational changes outlined above, the infantry of the British Army consisted of the following units:

1st (The Royal Scots) Regiment
2nd (The Queen's Royal) Regiment
3rd (East Kent – The Buffs) Regiment
4th (The King's Own Royal) Regiment
5th (Northumberland Fusiliers) Regiment
6th (Royal 1st Warwickshire) Regiment
7th (Royal Fusiliers) Regiment
8th (The King's) Regiment
9th (East Norfolk) Regiment
10th (The North Lincolnshire) Regiment
11th (North Devonshire) Regiment
12th (East Suffolk) Regiment
13th (1st Somersetshire) Prince Albert's Light Infantry Regiment
14th (The Buckinghamshire) Regiment (The Prince of Wales's Own)
15th (Yorkshire, East Riding) Regiment
16th (The Bedfordshire) Regiment
17th (The Leicestershire) Regiment
18th (The Royal Irish) Regiment
19th (1st Yorkshire, North Riding) Regiment (Princess of Wales's Own)
20th (The East Devonshire) Regiment
21st (Royal Scots Fusiliers) Regiment
22nd (The Cheshire) Regiment
23rd (Royal Welsh Fusiliers) Regiment
24th (The 2nd Warwickshire) Regiment
25th (The King's Own Borderers) Regiment
26th (The Cameronian) Regiment
27th (Inniskilling) Regiment
28th (North Gloucestershire) Regiment
29th (Worcestershire) Regiment
30th (The Cambridgeshire) Regiment
31st (The Huntingdonshire) Regiment
32nd (Cornwall) Light Infantry Regiment
33rd (Duke of Wellington's) Regiment
34th (The Cumberland) Regiment
35th (Royal Sussex) Regiment

36th (Herefordshire) Regiment
37th (North Hampshire) Regiment
38th (1st Staffordshire) Regiment
39th (The Dorsetshire) Regiment
40th (2nd Somersetshire) Regiment
41st (The Welsh) Regiment
42nd (The Royal Highland) Regiment (The Black Watch)
43rd (Monmouthshire Light Infantry) Regiment
44th (The East Essex) Regiment
45th (Nottinghamshire) Regiment (Sherwood Foresters)
46th (South Devonshire) Regiment
47th (Lancashire) Regiment
48th (Northamptonshire) Regiment
49th (Princess Charlotte of Wales's) (Herefordshire) Regiment
50th (The Queen's Own) Regiment
51st (2nd Yorkshire, West Riding) (The King's Own Light Infantry) Regiment
52nd (Oxfordshire) Light Infantry Regiment
53rd (Shropshire) Regiment
54th (West Norfolk) Regiment
55th (Westmoreland) Regiment
56th (West Essex) Regiment
57th (West Middlesex) Regiment
58th (Rutlandshire) Regiment
59th (2nd Nottinghamshire) Regiment
60th The King's Royal Rifle Corps
61st (South Gloucestershire) Regiment
62nd (Wiltshire) Regiment
63rd (West Suffolk) Regiment
64th (2nd Staffordshire) Regiment
65th (2nd Yorkshire, North Riding) Regiment
66th (Berkshire) Regiment
67th (South Hampshire) Regiment
68th (Durham) Light Infantry Regiment
69th (South Lincolnshire) Regiment
70th (Surrey) Regiment
71st (Highland) Light Infantry Regiment
72nd (Duke of Albany's Own Highlanders) Regiment
73rd (Perthshire) Regiment

74th (Highlanders) Regiment
75th (Stirlingshire) Regiment
76th Regiment of Foot
77th (East Middlesex/The Duke of Cambridge's Own) Regiment
78th (Highland) Regiment, (The Ross-shire Buffs)
79th (Queen's Own Cameron Highlanders) Regiment
80th (Staffordshire Volunteers) Regiment
81st (Loyal Lincoln Volunteers) Regiment
82nd (The Prince of Wales's Volunteers) Regiment
83rd (County Dublin) Regiment
84th (York and Lancaster) Regiment
85th (Bucks Volunteers) (The King's Light Infantry) Regiment
86th (Royal County Down) Regiment
87th (Royal Irish Fusiliers) Regiment
88th (Connaught Rangers) Regiment
89th (Princess Victoria's) Regiment
90th (Perthshire Volunteers – Light Infantry) Regiment
91st (Princess Louise's Argyllshire Highlanders) Regiment
92nd (Gordon Highlanders) Regiment
93rd (Sutherland Highlanders) Regiment
94th Regiment of Foot
95th (Derbyshire) Regiment
96th Regiment of Foot
97th (The Earl of Ulster's) Regiment
98th (Prince of Wales's) Regiment
99th (Duke of Edinburgh's/Lanarkshire) Regiment
100th (Prince of Wales's Royal Canadian) Regiment
101st (Royal Bengal Fusiliers) Regiment
102nd (Royal Madras Fusiliers) Regiment
103rd (Royal Bombay Fusiliers) Regiment
104th (Bengal Fusiliers) Regiment
105th (Madras Light Infantry) Regiment
106th (Bombay Light Infantry) Regiment
107th (Bengal Infantry) Regiment
108th (Madras Infantry) Regiment
109th (Bombay Infantry) Regiment
The Prince Consort's Own Rifle Brigade

Guard and Line Infantry 15

Musician of a Highland regiment in the 1820s, wearing a tail-coat with coloured frontal plastron. (*ASKB*)

As previously, the regiments defined as Fusiliers (nine in total) did not have any special feature. The same was valid for the eleven regiments named as Light Infantry, although the King's Royal Rifle Corps and Prince Consort's Own Rifle Brigade were proper light infantry units and had elite status. Between 1868 and 1874, the British Army underwent what was known as the Cardwell Reforms, which were sponsored by Liberal Prime Minister William Gladstone. These abolished the possibility of purchasing commissions in the army, in order to introduce new principles of meritocracy in all the branches of service of the military. Until that moment, most of the infantry and cavalry officers came from the landed gentry and were not promoted due to their personal capabilities. Real meritocracy could be found only in the ranks of the artillery and the technical corps, which could count on brilliant officers who had specific competences. Cardwell, as Secretary of State for War, did not intervene only with the officer corps, but also reformed several other aspects of military life. He abolished flogging and other harsh disciplinary measures in order to attract increasing numbers of good quality recruits. Furthermore, bounty money for recruits was abolished, together with all the other semi-illegal practices that were traditionally linked with recruiting operations. The military reforms of Cardwell were aimed at improving the general quality of the British Army, but also at reducing the

NCO of the Grenadier Guards wearing an M1831 tail-coat with epaulettes. (*ASKB*)

Officer of a light infantry regiment, wearing the M1828 shako and M1831 tail-coat. (*ASKB*)

Guard and Line Infantry 17

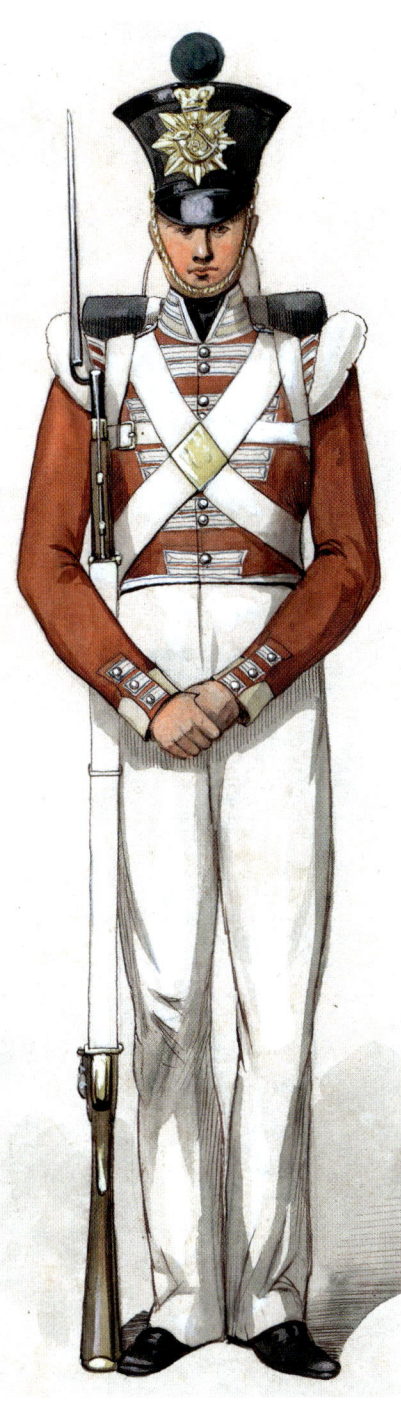

Line infantryman wearing an M1828 shako. The green pompom and the shoulder wings were distinctive of light companies. (*ASKB*)

financial costs deriving from the maintenance of the military. Garrisoning the overseas colonies, in particular, had enormous financial costs for the British finances; to deal with this problem, Cardwell sponsored the development of locally recruited military forces in the colonies that already had self-government in order to reduce the size of the garrisons deployed overseas. From 1869–71, the major British colonies – Canada, Australia and New Zealand – started organizing their own autonomous military structures, which permitted 26,000 British regulars to return home. Cardwell worked hard to create an Army Reserve that could support the active regiments in time of war, having learned from the experiences of recent European conflicts such as the Franco-Prussian War of 1870–71. He introduced what was known as short service, with the possibility for a soldier to abandon active service after just a few years (six for the infantry) in order to enter the ranks of the new Army Reserve. The Reserve was made up of part-time soldiers, who received reduced pay from the government in exchange for training each year for a short period of time and being ready to serve when called upon to do so (for example, in case of emergency). The new system introduced by Cardwell worked quite well, and by the end of Queen Victoria's reign there were 80,000 soldiers in the ranks of the Army Reserve, all still relatively young but with significant military experience. Until 1871, new recruits were liable to be drafted into any regiment regardless of their preference or geographical origin, another factor that made military service unpopular, which Cardwell eliminated by initiating the localization scheme. The territory of Great Britain was divided into

Officer of a Highland regiment wearing a feather bonnet and M1831 tail-coat. (*ASKB*)

sixty-six regimental districts, which were based on county boundaries and population density, each of which provided recruits to one or two infantry regiments. Cardwell, to carry on his process of localization, standardized the internal composition of the foot regiments, which started to consist of two battalions. One battalion was to serve overseas, while the other was stationed at home for training. The militia of each regimental district provided a third 'depot' battalion for each unit. The military reforms of Cardwell had a very positive impact on the British Army, which had changed very little since the glorious days of the Duke of Wellington.

The implementation of the new legislative measures, however, took a long time and was completed only under the new Secretary of State for War, Hugh Childers. The latter carried out a new and comprehensive reform of the British Army in 1881, according to which each regiment of foot was to consist of two active battalions and two militia battalions (three militia battalions for units recruited in Ireland). The years following the Crimean War had seen the flourishing of many volunteer military corps across Great Britain, which mostly derived from rifle associations and consisted of volunteers who wanted to perform home-defence on a part-time basis. Childers decided to regularize these volunteer corps that had emerged during the previous decades, by officially making them part of the British military. Each volunteer unit was associated by headquarters location and territorial name to its local regimental

Guard and Line Infantry 19

NCO of the 71st Foot (Highland Light Infantry) wearing the Highlanders' version of the M1828 shako and trews trousers. (*ASKB*)

district, in order to provide each regiment of foot with volunteer battalions. As a result of these organizational changes, each infantry regiment started to consist of two active battalions that were supported by two militia battalions (three in Ireland), plus a variable number of volunteer battalions. The two Rifle units of the British Army did not have regimental districts, since they were elite corps whose members came from every corner of Britain. Following the Childers Reforms, their affiliated militia and volunteer battalions were selected not on a territorial basis but due to their 'rifle' traditions (i.e., the best volunteer rifle corps were attached to the two regular Rifle units). Since many regiments of foot still consisted of just one battalion

Line infantrymen from the early months of the Crimean War.
They are all wearing the Albert shako with pompom in company colour.

Guard and Line Infantry 21

Officer (left) and private (right) of the line infantry fighting in Crimea. They both have the grey greatcoat that was worn during winter and the dark blue forage cap.

in 1881, Childers had to assemble together several of the existing units in order to have two battalions in each regiment. This caused great malcontent, especially among the most conservative officers and NCOs, who were proud of their regimental traditions. All the regiments of foot were renamed (except for a few of the oldest

NCO of the Grenadier Guards wearing the short-lived M1855 double-breasted tunic. (*ASKB*)

ones, which lobbied to retain their original denominations) and were deprived of their progressive number. Until 1881, as we will see, each infantry regiment had the facings of its uniform in a distinctive regimental colour. Childers, for reasons of economy and efficiency, abolished this practice and standardized facing colours: the regiments being designated as 'Royal' were assigned dark blue facings, the English and Welsh regiments white facings, the Scottish regiments yellow facings and the Irish regiments green facings. Distinctive national patterns were introduced for the lace of the officers' uniforms: a rose pattern for English and Welsh regiments, thistle for Scottish regiments and shamrock for Irish regiments. Lace was golden for the officers of the active battalions and silver for those of the militia and volunteer battalions. According to the Childers Reforms, the infantry of the British Army was restructured on a total of sixty-nine regiments (including the two Rifle units) as follows:

The Royal Scots (Lothian Regiment)
The Queen's (Royal West Surrey Regiment)
The Buffs (East Kent Regiment)
The King's Own (Royal Lancaster Regiment)
The Northumberland Fusiliers
The Royal Warwickshire Regiment
The Royal Fusiliers (City of London Regiment)
The Liverpool Regiment
The Norfolk Regiment
The Lincolnshire Regiment
The Devonshire Regiment
The Suffolk Regiment
Prince Albert's Light Infantry (Somersetshire Regiment)
The Prince of Wales's Own (West Yorkshire Regiment)
The East Yorkshire Regiment
The Bedfordshire Regiment
The Leicestershire Regiment
The Royal Irish Regiment
The Princess of Wales's Own (Yorkshire Regiment)
The Lancashire Fusiliers
The Royal Scots Fusiliers
The Cheshire Regiment
The Royal Welsh Fusiliers
The South Wales Borderers

The King's Own Borderers
The Cameronians (Scotch Rifles)
The Royal Inniskilling Fusiliers
The Gloucestershire Regiment
The Worcestershire Regiment
The West Lancashire Regiment
The East Surrey Regiment
The Duke of Cornwall's Light Infantry
The Duke of Wellington's (West Riding Regiment)
The Border Regiment
The Royal Sussex Regiment
The Hampshire Regiment
The South Staffordshire Regiment
The Dorsetshire Regiment
The Prince of Wales's Volunteers (South Lancashire Regiment)
The Welsh Regiment
The Black Watch (Royal Highlanders)
The Oxfordshire Light Infantry
The Essex Regiment
The Sherwood Foresters (Derbyshire Regiment)
The Loyal North Lancashire Regiment
The Northamptonshire Regiment
Princess Charlotte of Wales's (Berkshire Regiment)
The Queen's Own (Royal West Kent Regiment)
The King's Own Light Infantry (South Yorkshire Regiment)
The King's Light Infantry (Shropshire Regiment)
The Duke of Cambridge's Own (Middlesex Regiment)
The King's Royal Rifle Corps
The Duke of Edinburgh's (Wiltshire Regiment)
The Manchester Regiment
The Prince of Wales's (North Staffordshire Regiment)
The York and Lancaster Regiment
The Durham Light Infantry
The Highland Light Infantry
Seaforth Highlanders (Ross-shire Buffs)
The Gordon Highlanders
The Queen's Own Cameron Highlanders
The Royal Irish Rifles

The Royal Irish Fusiliers (Princess Victoria's)
The Connaught Rangers
Princess Louise's (Argyll and Sutherland Highlanders)
The Prince of Wales's Leinster Regiment (Royal Canadians)
The Royal Munster Fusiliers
The Royal Dublin Fusiliers
The Prince Consort's Own (Rifle Brigade)

Once again, the regiments defined as 'Fusiliers' (nine in total) did not have any special feature, nor did the seven regiments defined as 'Light Infantry', although the King's Royal Rifle Corps and Prince Consort's Own Rifle Brigade were still proper light infantry units with the associated elite status. The Scotch Rifles and Royal Irish Rifles were created to have at least one Rifle regiment each for Scotland and Ireland, but despite wearing dark green uniforms and having black leather equipment, these two units did not have the same superior tactical capabilities as the two 'true' Rifle corps. The infantry's general structure reported above did not see any major changes during the last years of Queen Victoria's reign, except for the fact that two extra active battalions were added to each of the following regiments after the outbreak of the Second Boer War: Northumberland Fusiliers, Warwickshire Regiment, Royal Fusiliers, Liverpool Regiment, Lancashire Fusiliers, Worcestershire Regiment, Middlesex Regiment and Manchester Regiment. The expansion of these units was made possible by the fact that their regimental districts included parts of large conurbations and thus had a growing population.

Since the mid-eighteenth century, the British line infantry had included several regiments of Highland infantry. These were not the only regiments of foot raised in Scotland, but differently from the units formed in the Scottish Lowlands (which were practically impossible to distinguish from their English equivalents) had peculiar military traditions and wore distinctive uniforms. The Lowlands had always been strongly linked with England and thus had accepted English rule in a quite favourable way, but the Highlands had remained very jealous of their freedom and had long opposed union with England. The Highlanders, who were widely acknowledged as the best fighters in the British Isles, rose up in revolt against the English several times during the eighteenth century, which prevented the authorities of the United Kingdom from raising regular military units from their warlike communities. After the Jacobite Rising of 1715, the British Army did not have the resources to leave a strong garrison in the Highlands, so was forced to keep order among the Highlanders by recruiting men from the local clans who were loyal to the British Crown. These new soldiers were employed mostly as rural policemen in order to deal with cattle

Officer (left), NCO (centre) and private (right) of the line infantry wearing the M1857 single-breasted tunic and French-pattern shako. (*ASKB*)

Guard and Line Infantry 27

Officer (left) and musician (right) of the light infantry wearing the M1857 single-breasted tunic and M1861 shako. (*ASKB*)

NCO (left) and ensign (right) of the line infantry wearing the M1868 tunic with pointed cuffs and M1869 shako. (*ASKB*)

rustling and other crimes that were typical of the Highlands during the eighteenth century. In 1725, the first units of these 'loyal' Highlanders were raised, known as the Independent Highland Companies. Their officers were commissioned by the British Army, while their men had only a semi-regular status and could not be considered proper soldiers. Independent Highland Companies had previously existed during the seventeenth century but had been disbanded in 1717; by reforming them, the British government hoped to maintain peace in the northern reaches of Scotland.

Officer (left) and musician (right) of the 71st Foot (Highland Light Infantry) in 1867. The officer is wearing the Highlanders' version of the M1861 shako and M1857 doublet tunic. (*ASKB*)

Initially, only three companies, with little more than 100 men in each, were raised, but another three companies of around seventy men each were later established. One company was recruited from members of Clan Munro, and others from Clan Fraser of Lovat, Clan Grant and Clan Campbell, the latter raising three such units. Collectively, the six companies were known as the Black Watch because of the dark colour of the tartan cloth with which their kilts were made. In 1739, another four companies were added to the corps, bringing the total to ten, and these were brought together to form the 42nd Regiment of Foot of the British Army (which was the first Highland regular unit to enter British service). The great success of the Black Watch, which distinguished itself in North America during the French-Indian War and the American Revolution, convinced the British to form several further Highland regiments during the second half of the eighteenth century. Generally speaking, the Highlanders were excellent soldiers: they could be less disciplined than their English compatriots, but their courage and fitness were unrivalled. They could defend a position to the last man and were extremely proud of their local traditions. On many occasions they were able to achieve success despite being in clear numerical inferiority, and their morale was usually very high. The Highlanders were used to existing in poor and rocky countryside, where living conditions were extremely harsh. They could thus endure hardships of any kind while on campaign, being able to manage for days with very little food. They were able to move very rapidly on every kind of terrain, meaning they had excellent skirmishing abilities that

Private of the 71st Foot (Highland Light Infantry) wearing the Highlanders' version of the M1861 shako and M1857 doublet tunic.

gave them a certain 'light infantry' character. In combat, the Highlanders were prone to using their bayonets much more frequently than the English regiments, retaining the fighting spirit of their ancient Celtic warrior forebears. Nevertheless, when needed, they could deliver very accurate fire upon enemy ranks. From an organizational point of view, the Highland regiments had exactly the same structure as the English ones, although one notable difference was that their musicians played bagpipes. By 1815, the following Highland regiments, eleven in total, were part of the British infantry:

42nd Regiment of Foot (Royal Highland)
71st Regiment of Foot (Glasgow Highland)
72nd Regiment of Foot (Seaforth Highlanders)
73rd Regiment of Foot
74th Regiment of Foot
75th Regiment of Foot
78th Regiment of Foot (Ross-Shire Buffs)
79th Regiment of Foot (Cameron Highlanders)
91st Regiment of Foot (Argyllshire Highlanders)
92nd Regiment of Foot (Gordon Highlanders)
93rd Regiment of Foot (Sutherland Highlanders)

In 1809, six of these units were ordered to wear 'trews' (trousers made of tartan cloth) instead of their traditional kilts, mostly for practical reasons, although this had no significant consequences for their Highland status. The five units that retained their kilts were the Royal Highland, Ross-Shire Buffs, Cameron Highlanders, Gordon Highlanders and Sutherland Highlanders. The decision to 'de-kilt' several Highland regiments was taken by the British authorities in the hope that it could make the Highland units more attractive to English recruits. Indeed, during the Napoleonic Wars, the Highland infantry units started to suffer from a chronic lack of recruits coming from the Scottish Highlands, and thus had to fill their ranks with individuals from other regions of Britain. In 1834, the Glasgow Highland Regiment was reissued with kilts. With the Childers Reforms of 1881, the existing Highland regiments were assembled as follows in order to form new units:

The 42nd Regiment and 73rd Regiment made up the new Black Watch (Royal Highlanders)

The 71st Regiment and 74th Regiment merged to become the new Highland Light Infantry

The 72nd Regiment and 78th Regiment became the new Seaforth Highlanders

The 91st Regiment and 93rd Regiment made up the new Argyll and Sutherland Highlanders

The 92nd Regiment and 75th Regiment became the new Gordon Highlanders

The 79th Regiment formed a second battalion and assumed the new denomination of the Queen's Own Cameron Highlanders

As a result of these organizational changes, the number of Highland regiments was reduced from eleven to six. The Scotch Rifles, which were formed as part of the Childers Reforms, wore trews but did not have Highland status.

Uniforms and Equipment

From 1797, the British line infantry wore a scarlet red tail-coat, which was single-breasted and had no lapels on the front. The tail-coat had false short tails on the back and horizontal back-pockets for the centre/grenadier companies (the light infantry companies had oblique back-pockets). On the front, the tail-coat had five couples of buttons, while four buttons were placed on each cuff and pocket. All twenty-six buttons had white lace, while the standing collar of the tail-coat was piped in white. Both the collar and the round cuffs were in the distinctive colour of each regiment, as well as the shoulder straps, which were also piped in white. All the regiments bearing the title 'Royal' in their official denomination (and the Foot Guards) had dark blue as their facing colour. The shoulder straps had a white crest where they were sewn to the shoulder and were pointed at the other end (where they were secured, close to the collar, by a small button). Flank companies did not have shoulder straps like these but peculiar shoulder wings, which were edged in white and padded with white wool. The light infantry units included among the regiments of foot were dressed like the line infantry corps, but had shoulder wings for all their companies. The tail-coats of the Highland regiments were slightly different from those of the other units, having just four couples of buttons on the front and three buttons on each pocket; in addition, all companies of the Highland regiments had oblique pockets. Infantry officers wore a scarlet red double-breasted tail-coat having frontal lapels in regimental colour; these, from 1815, started to be buttoned up in order to look like a plastron. The musicians of each line infantry regiment wore the same uniform as the other soldiers, but with reversed colours: the tail-coat was in the distinctive colour of each regiment, while the facings were scarlet red. All the musicians' tail-coats were laced on the seams, the colour and decorative design of the distinctive lace being chosen by the commander of each regiment and thus being different for each unit. The musicians' tail-coats were also decorated with strips of cloth (usually having a 'V' shape) that were worn on the sleeves and had the same colour/decorative design as the seams' lace. In 1831, the practice of having the musicians dressed in reversed colours was abandoned. The infantry's tail-coat was worn with dark grey trousers during cold months and white trousers during hot months. The Highland regiments used their traditional kilts, which were produced with a distinctive kind of tartan cloth for each unit. On the front of their kilts, the Highlanders wore the characteristic sporran pouch and usually carried a sgian-dubh single-edged knife. Together with the ordinary line infantry's black shoes, the Highlanders also wore their traditional hose socks that were made from white-and-red tartan for all regiments. During the Napoleonic Wars, as we have seen, several Highland regiments were ordered to replace their kilts with trousers made from tartan cloth (trews).

In March 1812, a new model of shako was introduced for the British line infantry, which later became known as Belgian or Waterloo shako, since it was used during the Belgian campaign of 1815. The main feature of this headgear was that it had a crown

NCO (left), officer (centre) and private (right) of the line infantry wearing the M1878 spiked helmet and M1868 tunic. (*ASKB*)

Officer (left) and private (right) of the line infantry wearing the M1878 spiked helmet and M1868 tunic. (*ASKB*)

that sloped down at the back, producing a false front. On the rear, the crown was also a bit broader. It was made of black felt for rankers; for NCOs it was produced with coarse beaver, while for officers it was made from fine beaver. The false front was edged with black lace, and on the front of the shako there was a peak made of lacquered leather. An additional band of black lace was frequently worn around the bottom part of the headgear, especially by officers. The M1812 shako had a feather tuft for officers and a worsted tuft for other ranks, in the distinctive colour of each company (half-white and half-red for centre companies, white for grenadier companies and green for light companies). The tuft was worn on the left side of the shako, and at the base of the tuft there was a black cockade, held in place by a button. The latter bore the regimental number for centre companies, a flaming grenade for grenadier companies and a bugle horn for light infantry companies. On the front of the shako was a twist cord with a tassel at each end; a doubled loop knot was formed to shorten the cord into two lengths, with an un-knotted length at the centre. The cord was worn with the doubled loop end hooked behind the cockade, with the two lengths of loop knots either side of the shako plate and the two tassels on the right. This cord was golden for officers, white for centre and grenadier companies, and green for light companies. The frontal plate of the M1812 shako was made of copper-gilt for officers and brass for other ranks. The standard badge reproduced on it comprised a crown in the top part, a British royal cypher in the centre and the regimental number at the bottom. The Foot Guards, the 'Royal' regiments and some other units wore their distinctive symbols on the frontal plate. From December 1814, the light infantry regiments and the light companies of the line regiments were ordered to replace the frontal plates of their shakos with two separate badges: one with a bugle horn and the other the unit number. Both were usually of silver colour. Officially, grenadiers could wear a black bearskin as an alternative to the shako, but this was used only on parade during the Napoleonic Wars and was abolished in 1844. The Grenadier Guards – from 1815 – were the only regiment to retain the bearskin as the headgear for all its companies, and continued to use it throughout the nineteenth century. The grenadier companies of the regiments defined as 'Fusiliers' had the privilege of wearing fur caps on parade until the end of Queen Victoria's reign.

The standard headgear of the Highland regiments was the feather bonnet, which was dark blue and could be fitted with a removable peak on the front if required. Around the feather bonnet was a chequered band of white, red and green or one of white and red known as Sutherland dicing. On the back of the bonnet were two black tails, which went over the neck, while on the top was a pompom (known as a 'tourie') made of wool, which was white for grenadiers, red for fusiliers and green for light companies. In addition, as is clear from its denomination, the headgear

Officer (left) and NCO (right) of the 42nd Regiment of Foot (Black Watch) wearing a feather bonnet and M1868 doublet tunic with gauntlet-shaped cuffs. (*ASKB*)

Guard and Line Infantry 37

Officers (left), musicians (centre) and NCO (right) of the 42nd Regiment of Foot (Black Watch) wearing a feather bonnet and M1868 doublet tunic with gauntlet-shaped cuffs.

Officer (left) and NCO (right) of the 71st Regiment of Foot (Highland Light Infantry) wearing the Highlanders' version of the M1869 shako and M1868 doublet tunic with gauntlet-shaped cuffs. (*ASKB*)

had decorative black ostrich feathers that covered most of its body. These feathers, which were sewn around the stiff blue cloth of the cap, were of two different kinds combined together: the shorter 'flats' and the longer 'foxtails'. The foxtails curved over the flats and provided the required fullness of the headgear. The feathers (clipped and fastened on a stem) were worn on the left side of the bonnet and were held in position by a black cockade, which had a metal button that bore the regimental number for centre companies, a flaming grenade for grenadier ones and a bugle horn for light companies. A coloured plume was applied on the left side of the bonnet. This was held in place by the black cockade and was white for grenadier companies, white-over-red for centre companies and green for light companies. The plumes of flank companies were longer than those of battalion companies. The 42nd Regiment of Foot was the only one to have different colours for the plume: entirely red for fusiliers, red-over-white for grenadiers and red-over-green for light companies. On campaign, a flat version of the headgear was frequently worn. Known as a 'hummel' bonnet, this was dark blue and bore the black cockade near the tourie, but had no tails on the back and no chequered band or feathers.

In 1816, a new model of shako was introduced, replacing the previous Belgian version. This was known as the Regency shako because it was distributed to the British line infantry during the Regency era (1811–20). This new headgear had the shape of an inverted cone and was made of black felt, but its top was covered with black leather. Two peaks were attached to the shako, the rear one being much less deep than the front peak. Bands of lace – either yellow or white, depending on the regimental officers' lace colour, which could be golden or silver – circled the top of the headgear. An additional band of the same colour was placed around the bottom edge, just above the peaks. The black cockade (a symbol of the House of Hanover) was placed at the centre front of the shako, with a regimental button in the middle. Arising from the cockade was a worsted wool plume in the same company colours as the M1812 shako. The frontal plate had a new design, which featured a regimental-numbered disc surmounted by a crown, and was linked to the cockade placed above it by brass scales. Light companies and light infantry regiments had a bugle badge in place of the plate. The shako was secured to the head by brass lion-head bosses and chin scales. The 2nd Foot Guards and 3rd Foot Guards, differently from the 1st Foot Guards, had the shako as their headgear; they used it with a distinctive frontal plate (in the shape of a star) and without top or bottom lace. This headgear was never particularly popular, and was abolished in 1822. In 1831, the Coldstream Guards and Scots Guards were assigned bearskins, abandoning the use of the shako. From 1822, all the companies of the Highland regiments started to have shoulder wings instead of the standard shoulder-straps. In 1828, a new model of shako was introduced, which was more bell-shaped than the previous one. In 1835, the shako's plume was replaced by a pompom in company colour.

The tail-coat of the line infantry underwent no significant modifications until 1831, when for guard units and officers of the line units it started to have two close rows of buttons down the front and cuff flaps having four buttons each (the latter had already been adopted by the guard infantry since 1822). The cuff flaps of the new tail-coat were scarlet red and their buttonholes were laced in white, but the front of the tail-coat had no white lace on the buttonholes. From 1836, the new double-breasted tail-coat (which had epaulettes) was also adopted by sergeants, although the rankers of the line units continued to wear their usual single-breasted tail-coat with white lace loops on the buttonholes until 1855. In 1836, the previous regimental patterns for the lacing of buttonholes were replaced by plain white loops that were identical for all regiments. Until the late 1830s, the Highland regiments wore the feather bonnet – also known as the Kilmarnock bonnet, from the place where it originated – as their main headgear. From the late 1830s, however, they started to wear their own version of the line infantry shako as an alternative to the Kilmarnock. The Highlanders' version of the shako was dark blue and had a hand-knitted diced band around the bottom. Indeed, all the models of shako used by the British regiments of foot from 1838–78 were produced in a specific dark blue version for the Highlanders. The only Highland light regiment – the 71st Regiment of Foot – wore the dark blue shako on all occasions.

In 1844, the new Albert shako was introduced to replace the previous M1828 one, its name deriving from the fact that it was originally designed by Prince Albert, the husband of Queen Victoria. Compared with the previous bell-top shako, the new one was taller, being cylindrical in shape and tapering inwards. The Albert shako was made of felt and had two leather peaks (at the front and at the rear). The brass frontal plate was circular (star-shaped for officers) and bore the regimental number under a crown. Light companies and light infantry regiments had a bugle reproduced in the centre of the plate, while grenadier companies had a grenade. A coloured pompom placed at the front of the top and a black leather chinstrap completed the Albert shako, the pompom being in company colour like the plume of the M1828 shako (half-red and half-white for centre companies, white for grenadier companies and green for light infantry companies). For officers only, the chinstrap was covered with a gilt chain that was fixed to the side of the shako with gilt rosettes. On campaign, for example during the opening battles of the Crimean War, the shako was often replaced by a round forage cap. This dark blue cap was extremely comfortable to wear and bore a brass regimental number on the front. From 1846, the British line infantry used dark blue trousers with red side-stripe during cold months and white trousers

Officers of the Grenadier Guards wearing the M1881 tunic. (*ASKB*)

during hot months. The winter trousers were not modified until the end of the century, while use of the summer trousers was later restricted only to overseas service.

In 1855, the old-fashioned tail-coat was replaced with an innovative double-breasted tunic. This was scarlet red with standing collar and round cuffs in regimental colour; both the collar and the cuffs were piped in white. Cuff flaps were in regimental colour and had three buttons each, no lace on the buttonholes and were piped in white. During the first phase of the Crimean War, the British infantry wore tail-coats, but later in the conflict they were dressed in the new M1855 tunic. The latter had white piping on the front and shoulder straps in regimental colour (which had white piping and bore a white regimental number). When the British line infantry adopted this tunic in 1855, a new garment had to be designed for the Highlanders, as their kilts were not compatible with the double-breasted tunic. As a result, a new jacket

Private (left) and officer (right) of the Coldstream Guards wearing the M1881 tunic. (*ASKB*)

known as a doublet came into use, which, instead of skirts, had four pieces known as Inverness flaps. Each of these flaps had three buttons and three buttonholes laced in white. In 1855, the Albert shako was replaced by a new headgear, known as a French-pattern shako since it resembled the kepi worn by the contemporary French army of Napoleon III. The new shako was much shorter than the previous headgear, having a forward-pointing shape, black leather chinstrap, and front and rear peak and top and bottom band all made of black leather. The brass frontal plate bore the regimental number under a crown, and the shako was completed by a pompom in company colour. The M1855 tunic was quite short-lived, since in 1857 it was slightly modified and became single-breasted (the doublet of the Highlanders was also amended to be single-breasted). In 1861, the French-pattern shako was slightly modified, becoming shorter and being deprived of the top band in black leather, in order to resemble more closely a kepi. In 1868, cuff flaps were abolished for all line regiments and the round cuffs were replaced by new pointed ones (always in regimental colour, being gauntlet-shaped for the Highlanders). The standing collar became red with a patch in regimental colour, which bore a brass unit number; the Highland units had no collar patch. In 1869, the shako worn by the British line infantry was modified again, completing its slow transformation into a kepi. The M1869 shako was made of dark blue cloth (green for the regiments defined as light infantry) and had a black leather

From left to right: musician, private, musician, officers and NCO of the Cameron Highlanders wearing the feather bonnet and M1881 tunic. (*ASKB*)

peak as well as brass chin scales. The pompom remained the same, while the brass frontal plate started to consist of a round badge bearing the regimental number, which was surrounded by laurel branches and surmounted by a crown. The officers' headgear had golden quarter-piping to show their rank.

In 1878, the British line infantry adopted a new model of headgear, which soon became iconic, which consisted of a black spiked helmet, which had a brass spike on top and brass chin scales (departing from a brass rosette on each side of the headgear). The new helmet had a brass plate on the front, which bore the distinctive motto and symbol of each regiment under a crown. The spiked helmet was also used by the Highlanders as an alternative to the feather bonnet. On campaign and overseas, the M1878 headgear was always replaced by a much simpler cork helmet (better known now as a pith helmet), which was covered with white cotton cloth. The cork helmet could have brass chin scales and frontal plate, but on most occasions these were removed for campaign use. In 1881, the single-breasted tunic of the line infantry was modified, in order to carry on a general simplification of the British Army's dress. The tunic became shorter, but continued to have white piping on the front and Inverness flaps for the Highlanders. Shoulder straps were now in regimental colour, with white piping and brass unit number. The cuffs became round with cuff flaps instead of pointed, but the flaps were worn only with parade dress. Facing colours were standardized: the regiments designated as 'Royal' (including the 'Guards') were assigned dark blue facings, while the English and Welsh regiments were assigned white facings, the Scottish regiments had yellow facings and the Irish regiments received green facings. Distinctive national patterns were introduced for the lace of the officers' uniforms: a rose pattern for English and Welsh regiments, thistle for Scottish regiments and shamrock for Irish regiments. Lace was golden for the officers of the active battalions, silver for those of the militia and volunteer battalions. Trousers were not modified by the dress regulations of 1881, remaining valid until the end of Queen Victoria's reign, but only for parade use.

From 1846, some military units raised by the British in India were dressed in khaki, a word derived from a term of the Urdu language meaning 'soil-coloured'. Khaki clothes were relatively cheap to produce but extremely comfortable to wear on campaign. Consequently, it became common practice for British regular units serving in India (for example during the Indian Mutiny) to replace their usual red dress with khaki uniforms. These provided an early form of camouflaging and were produced with light cotton cloth. Most of the British troops taking part in the Second Anglo-Afghan War of 1878–80 wore khaki campaign jackets and trousers, as well as cork helmets covered with khaki cloth. From 1881, khaki became the official service dress in India. It was dyed on a regimental basis, with various kinds of pigments –

Guard and Line Infantry 45

Line infantryman from the Second Boer War wearing khaki campaign dress. (*ASKB*)

Private of the Gordon Highlanders from the Second Boer War wearing khaki campaign dress. (*ASKB*)

from tea and coffee to mud and curry powder – being used to produce campaign uniforms. Initially, the British were reluctant to adopt khaki for the units serving outside India. For the 1882 campaign in Egypt, for example, the various units sent to North Africa were assigned grey campaign dress. During the Sudan campaign of 1897–98, however, all the British troops operating in Africa were issued with khaki uniforms. These officially became the universal service dress of the British Army during the Second Boer War, which was the last major war fought during Queen Victoria's long reign.

As for weapons, until 1842 the British line infantry was equipped with the famous Brown Bess flintlock musket that was extensively used during the Napoleonic Wars. The Brown Bess was replaced by the Pattern 1842 musket, which was a percussion-lock conversion of the Brown Bess. The Pattern 1842 musket was replaced during the crucial years of the Crimean War by the Pattern 1853 Enfield rifle, which was the first rifle weapon used by the British line infantry. The Enfield remained in service until 1866, when the new Snider-Enfield rifle came into use, a breech-loading conversion of the Pattern 1853 Enfield and itself the first breech-loading weapon used by the British line infantry. In 1871, the robust Martini-Henry was adopted as the standard weapon of the British infantry, remaining in service until 1888, when it started to be replaced by the superior Lee-Metford. This, despite being produced from 1892 in a new version that incorporated a ten-round detachable box magazine, was substituted in 1895 by the Lee-Enfield rifle that was the standard British infantry weapon during the First World War.

Chapter 2

Rifles and Light Infantry

History and Organization

The Seven Years' War of 1756–63 involved the clash between Great Britain and France not only in Europe but also in their overseas colonies, most notably in North America, where the British controlled the Thirteen Colonies and France ruled over Canada. In North America, the tactical situations experienced by the British Army were completely different from those in Europe. The terrain of the Thirteen Colonies, as well as that of French Canada, was mostly covered with dense forests and inhabited by native communities whose warriors fought as lightly armed and highly mobile skirmishers. Colonial warfare in North America consisted of rapid raids and incursions launched across the frontier; as a result, each British or French colonist/farmer was also a militiaman skilled at skirmishing. In order to survive, each settler had to learn to hunt in the forests and fight against the natives by using their same methods of war. In the late seventeenth century, the first great war in the history of Colonial America was fought between the English colonists and the native tribes. This conflict, which broke out in 1675, is commonly known as King Philip's War, from the nickname that the colonists gave to their main native opponent (a great leader whose actual name was Metacomet). The war consisted of a native uprising that took place along the borders of the English colonies, which it was feared could lead to the expulsion of the whites from that part of North America. Using hit-and-run guerrilla tactics, the native warriors of Metacomet caused many losses to the colonial militia and destroyed a large number of English settlements. Learning from experience, the colonists understood that they must create a light infantry corps that could oppose the native attacks by using the same tactics as Metacomet. Command of this new experimental unit was given to Benjamin Church, a settler with extensive combat experience in the woods. The single company of this new corps were known as rangers. During the second half of the conflict, Church's men obtained a series of victories over the natives and finally killed Metacomet during a skirmish, a key factor behind the final victory of the colonists.

From 1675, all the English colonies of North America started to have their own units of rangers, which were deployed along the frontier with the native territories:

Rifles and Light Infantry 49

NCO of the King's Royal Rifle Corps wearing jacket with black frontal frogging and Regency shako with black drooping plume.

light infantry were thus effectively born in the New World. What had been achieved in North America, however, was not learned in Europe. No English troops had participated in King Philip's War, and Benjamin Church's innovations did not reach Europe. At the beginning of the eighteenth century, the American Colonies were considered a secondary theatre of operations by the British Army, a situation that did not change until the outbreak of the Seven Years' War (which was called French-Indian War in North America, where it began two years before the start of hostilities in Europe). During this conflict, the British Army had to intervene in the Thirteen Colonies with substantial contingents of troops in order to counter the expansionist ambitions of the French, who had formed political alliances with most of the native tribes and controlled the fur trade of North America. The French colonists were all potential light infantrymen, since they were not farmers like the British colonists but hunters who lived in close contact with the native tribes. After raids launched by the French militiamen and their natives allies resulted in a series of massacres of British settlers, it became apparent that the ranger units already existing in North America had to be expanded with the creation of new light infantry corps. As a result, several ranger units

Officer of the King's Royal Rifle Corps wearing hussar-style dress and M1828 shako. (*ASKB*)

were organized, but they remained provincial in nature, raised only for service in the Americas, and were not included in the official establishment of the British Army. In 1756, however, it was finally decided to create the first regular light infantry unit of the British Army. This was largely as a result of a disastrous defeat suffered by the British line infantry in 1754 at the Battle of Monogahela, where 1,300 British soldiers were ambushed and annihilated by a smaller force of Frenchmen and natives.

The new light infantry unit created after the Battle of Monogahela was initially known as the 62nd 'Royal American' Regiment of Foot, only adopting its definitive progressive number (the 60th) at a later date. Approval and funds for the raising of the new regiment were granted by the British Parliament in late 1755. The new unit comprised four battalions, each 1,000-strong, its main function being to deal with the raids launched by the French and their native allies against the settlements of the Thirteen Colonies. The regiment was recruited from colonists who already had experience of light infantry tactics, as well as foreigners who had hunting abilities. In particular, the British Army was interested in recruiting German hunters and gamekeepers, like those who were already serving in the light corps of the Prussian and French armies. In 1756, Parliament passed the Commissions to Foreign Protestants Act that permitted the recruiting of foreign officers from the German states and Swiss cantons. These men were employed in the new 62nd Regiment of Foot, but could not rise above the rank of lieutenant colonel. In total, some fifty officers of the new regiment came from Germany or Switzerland, but overall command of the unit was given to General John Campbell (then commander-in-chief of the British Army in North America). The original idea for the formation of the new unit came from Jacques Prevost, a Swiss soldier and adventurer who was a personal friend of the Duke of Cumberland (second son of George II). Prevost was an expert in forest warfare and one of the first to understand the combat potential of light infantry. In general terms, the Royal American Regiment united the main features of provincial (colonial) and foreign (mercenary) corps, merging the light infantry traditions of North America (as expressed by the rangers) with those of Central Europe (the jagers, or hunters, of the German armies). All members of the new unit were Protestants, their direct opponents being French Catholics. The foreign officers of the regiment included two notable personalities: Henri Bouquet (who commanded the 1st Battalion) and Frederick Haldimand (in charge of the 2nd Battalion). These two Swiss professional soldiers made a great contribution to the development of light infantry doctrines within the British Army. Their forward-looking ideas included the introduction (initially only unofficially) of rifled muskets among the rankers, these new weapons, which had long barrels and spiralled grooves in the bore, having started to be produced on a small scale during the early eighteenth century. They had become popular in the American colonies thanks to the German gunsmiths who migrated to the New World and brought these new muskets with them. Thanks to their superior precision, the rifles were an ideal weapon for hunting and fighting in the woods of North America, being gradually adopted by all the colonists and militiamen of the Thirteen Colonies. This superior flintlock weapon, however, was not adopted by the armies of Europe for many years, and continued to be used only for hunting. During the Seven Years' War, some of the newly formed light corps of the European armies started to adopt rifled carbines, more or less at the same time as a number of soldiers from the Royal American Regiment began substituting their smoothbores with rifled muskets. The production costs of the rifles were still quite high, but using such a weapon could determine the outcome of a battle due to its high level of accuracy. The French-Indian War was the first conflict during which rifles were used on a large scale, but it would take another ninety years before the adoption of rifled muskets by the line infantry. Bouquet and Haldimand also modified the standard uniforms of the British line infantry, in order to make them more comfortable for light infantry use. The long tails of the coat were shortened to increase mobility, and for practicality the coloured frontal lapels started to be buttoned up. During the French-Indian War, the 60th Regiment of Foot earned a solid combat reputation and the motto '*Celer et Audax*' ('Swift and Bold'). In 1762, in order to keep its soldiers in the ranks of the British armed forces, Parliament passed the American Protestant Soldier Naturalization Act, which offered naturalization to all those foreign officers and soldiers who had already served under the Union Jack for at least two years.

During the American Revolution of 1775–83, the 3rd and 4th Battalions of the 60th Regiment of Foot were brought back to their original establishments, having been reduced for several years. This was done by recruiting new soldiers from Britain and Hanover. The German state was in a 'personal union' with the British Crown during the period 1714–1837, being an independent nation but having as its head of state the King of Great Britain (the Hanover family having ruled the Kingdom of Great Britain since 1714). Hanover therefore provided a large number of expert German hunters and gamekeepers to the 60th Regiment of Foot, which fought with distinction during the American Revolution and remained loyal to the Crown despite comprising large numbers of American privates. During the war, it was an example to follow for many of the new provincial units of loyalists that were raised in North America in order to support the British Army. Many of these new corps were light infantry, equipped with rifled weapons, performing auxiliary duties for the British and being of great use to them since they were made up of colonists who had great experience of fighting in the forests (most of them being veterans of the provincial

Rifles and Light Infantry 53

Officer of the Rifle Brigade wearing an M1831 jacket and Albert shako.

units raised during the French-Indian War). Upon the conclusion of the American Revolution, all the loyalist corps were disbanded. But the 60th Regiment of Foot continued to serve in the British Army, remaining its only light unit for several years. The 5th Battalion was raised in 1797 by using the soldiers of a German mercenary regiment (Hompesch's Mounted Riflemen) that had recently been disbanded. The

6th Battalion was added in 1799, comprising German recruits. Finally, another two battalions were raised in 1813 for service in the Americas during the War of 1812 against the United States. These last two battalions were recruited from German and Swiss prisoners of war who had fought for Napoleon. The 60th Regiment of Foot continued to be strongly linked to the Americas during the Napoleonic Wars and remained the British foot regiment with the highest percentage of German/Swiss rankers. Of the eight battalions that made up the unit, only the 5th, raised in 1797, was entirely armed with rifles, the original four each having just one company

Private (left) and officers (right) of the Rifle Brigade. The private is wearing an M1831 jacket and Albert shako, while the officers are wearing service dress. (*ASKB*)

equipped with rifled carbines. The 6th Battalion, established in 1799, had just one company armed with rifles, while the last two battalions formed in 1813 had two rifle companies each. From 1797, the rifle units of the British light infantry started to be dressed in dark green, so this colour was worn by the entire 5th Battalion and the rifle companies of the other formations. The remaining companies, armed with smoothbores, continued to wear the standard scarlet red uniforms.

During the American Revolution, the British Army had to face the 'minutemen', the militiamen of the Thirteen Colonies who were able to form their companies and fight in just one minute if needed. These irregular fighters were all armed with rifled muskets – known as 'Kentucky rifles' – and were skilled skirmishers, being excellent marksmen and knowing how to conceal themselves in the woods. They caused serious troubles to the British line infantry, especially during the first phase of the conflict, when they always avoided fighting in the open field and were able to move much more rapidly than their opponents. In 1758, each British line battalion had been ordered to train one of its companies as light infantry, but this measure was abolished with the end of the Seven Years' War. In 1771, a single light company was reintroduced in all the line battalions, but this measure had not yet been properly implemented when the conflict in the Thirteen Colonies began. As a result, to counter the minutemen, the British had to rely almost entirely on the rangers and light corps organized by the American loyalists. The British Army could also employ its Highland regiments as light infantry units, since the Scottish fighters frequently had all the characteristics of excellent light infantrymen. With the end of the bloody American conflict, all the loyalist light corps were disbanded, together with the temporary battalions that had been formed by assembling together light companies from different regiments. The British infantry was greatly reduced in numbers, but the lessons learned about light infantry fighting were not completely forgotten; one light company was retained in all battalions, this measure being confirmed by the new organizational regulations that were enacted in 1792. However, the British light infantry still had their limitations, largely due to their soldiers being armed with flintlock smoothbores. In addition, the prejudices of the more traditionalist officers towards light infantry were still strong. As a result of this situation, during the Revolutionary Wars with France, the British Army had to rely on the recruiting of foreign and mercenary regiments from continental Europe in order to have enough light infantrymen. These formations were usually short-lived and were never considered to be a significant component of the British military. This situation changed only with the progression of the Revolutionary Wars, during which the French light infantry showed its mastery on several occasions. The British eventually understood that a general reform was urgently needed if their armies were to face the French chasseurs on anything like equal terms. The first step in this direction was taken in 1798, when the Duke of York authorized the publication of the Regulations for the Exercise of Riflemen and Light Infantry. These were written by the commander of the 60th Regiment of Foot's 5th Battalion and were the first manual for the light infantry of the British Army. Their publication marked the beginning of an important debate that took place within the officer corps: the more traditionalist officers were against the creation of new independent regiments of light infantry and still considered the formation of temporary light battalions as the best way to have light troops when needed; the more innovative officers wanted to select the fittest and most intelligent officers and rankers from all the existing line regiments in order to create new light infantry units. In the end, the innovators prevailed, aided by the victories of Revolutionary France having isolated Britain from the rest of Europe and made the recruiting of mercenary light infantrymen from the continent virtually impossible.

Consequently, in January 1800, each of the following line regiments was required to provide one captain, one lieutenant, one ensign, two sergeants, one corporal and thirty of its best privates in order to be trained as riflemen: 1st, 21st, 23rd, 25th, 27th, 29th, 49th, 69th, 71st, 72nd, 79th, 85th and 92nd. The chosen men, who were the best marksmen of their respective units, made up a new independent corps of riflemen. It is

Officer of the King's Royal Rifle Corps wearing an M1857 tunic with black frontal frogging and French-pattern shako. (*ASKB*)

interesting to note that several of the selected regiments were Highland ones, since they already had a light infantry status and were famed for the hardiness of their men. The initial idea was to train these elite soldiers as riflemen and send them back to their original units in order to act as the core for the formation of rifle companies in each line regiment. The newly created temporary training unit was known as the Experimental Corps of Riflemen and was commanded by Colonel Coote Manningham (one of the best light infantry officers in the British Army). He trained the riflemen by following his innovative ideas, which were published in 1800 as the *Regulations for the Rifle Corps Formed at Blachington Barracks under the Command of Colonel Manningham*. Members of the Experimental Corps of Riflemen were trained to react with rigid and unthinking obedience to the orders received, in order to be more autonomous on the battlefield and create a special relationship with their officers and NCOs that was based on mutual trust. A new sense of comradeship was developed, and one 'soldier of merit' was selected in each half-platoon to assume command of his squad in the absence of NCOs and be in a privileged position to be promoted as corporal. The Experimental Corps of Riflemen comprised a total of just five companies, each of which was divided into two equal-sized platoons, which were in turn split into four squads. The members of each squad trained and lived together every day, developing a special bond that would be of great use on the battlefield. Meritocracy was encouraged in every possible way, including prizes offered by the officers to the best marksmen who were under their command. Training of the new experimental corps was very intensive, comprising of field exercises that were made as realistic as possible. The basic idea was to forge soldiers who could think independently and act rapidly according to circumstances. Individual capabilities were fundamental, and thus only the best soldiers of the British infantry were admitted to the ranks of the Experimental Corps of Riflemen.

Training included moving swiftly on broken terrain, surviving with the few food resources that an enemy countryside could offer, skirmishing on the open field, penetrating the enemy's lines without being noticed, launching surprise attacks to occupy enemy outposts, scouting for larger units and acting as a rearguard to cover a retreat. From the beginning, the new riflemen were given dark green uniforms and black leather equipment. In August 1800, after just a few months of effective training, three companies of the Experimental Corps of Riflemen joined an amphibious expedition launched against the Spanish arsenal of Ferrol. Although the mission ended in failure, the companies of riflemen fought with great competence and covered the retreat of the line infantrymen. After the return of the three companies that had fought in Spain, new recruits were added to the Rifle Corps (the new denomination being introduced in October 1800). The unit could thus be expanded to become a battalion. In February 1801, it was transferred to the official establishment of the infantry and became a permanent unit. Then in 1802, it was officially transformed into a regiment and became the 95th Rifle Regiment. During the following years, the riflemen took part in all the major campaigns fought by the British Army, always distinguishing themselves and winning an impressive number of awards. Due to their superior training and morale, they were usually employed as 'special forces', accomplishing missions that seemed impossible on paper. In 1805, a 2nd Battalion was added to the Rifle Regiment, which was followed by a 3rd Battalion in 1809.

The early success of the Rifles encouraged the British high command to implement its light infantry reforms by transforming several of the existing line regiments. The main supporter of this process was General Sir John Moore, who was ordered to retrain the 52nd and 43rd Regiments of Foot as light units. Moore was the commander of the 52nd Regiment of Foot and had long been one of the officers who wished to expand the light component of the British infantry. In 1803, the two regiments were transferred to the training camp of the Rifles at Shorncliffe in Kent, where they trained together with members of the 95th Rifle Regiment and were gradually transformed into light infantry. This change did not change their internal structure, which continued to be based on battalions, but did affect their tactics and combat doctrines. The new light infantrymen retained their red uniforms and continued to be armed with smoothbore muskets (albeit of a special 'light' version), but learned how to fight in open order and to act as skirmishers. From then on, the British Army started to comprise two distinct components of light foot troops: the elite Rifles – who were armed with rifled carbines and were mostly employed as special forces – and the light infantrymen of the converted regiments, who were equipped with smoothbore muskets but trained as light skirmishers. The methods of training employed by Moore were very similar to those introduced by Manningham in 1800, which were based on the *Regulations for the Exercise of Riflemen and Light Infantry* published some time before by the commander of the 60th Regiment's 5th Battalion (the Swiss Baron de Rottenburg, a light infantry expert). In September 1805, the retraining of the 43rd and 52nd Regiments of Foot was completed, and both units were later sent to the Iberian Peninsula. Here, together with most of the 95th Rifles and some allied units, they formed a special Light Division that acted as a special corps for Wellington. Following the operational success of the 43rd and 52nd Regiments of Foot, more line infantry units were transformed into light regiments during the Napoleonic Wars. By 1815, the following regiments of the British infantry had become 'light' ones:

Rifles and Light Infantry 59

51st Regiment of Foot (transformed in 1809)
68th Regiment of Foot (transformed in 1808)
71st Regiment of Foot (transformed in 1809)
85th Regiment of Foot (transformed in 1808)

Private (left) and NCOs (right) of the Rifle Brigade.
Two of the figures are wearing the M1873 busby and M1868 tunic. (*ASKB*)

90th Regiment of Foot (transformed in 1815)

As a result, by the end of the Napoleonic period, the British Army included one regiment of rifles with three battalions (the 95th), one mixed regiment of rifles/light infantry with eight battalions (the 60th) and seven regiments of light infantry that were former line units. During the post-Napoleonic period, another two line regiments were transformed into light units: the 13th Regiment of Foot in 1822 and 32nd Regiment of Foot in 1858, meaning that, by 1860, there were nine light infantry regiments in the British Army. These became almost impossible to distinguish from the line regiments after the Napoleonic Wars, using the same weapons as the line infantry and wearing the same scarlet red uniforms (except for a few details, as described in the previous chapter). The internal organization of the light units was also exactly the same as for line regiments, but the light infantrymen continued to undergo specific training that enabled them to fight in open order as skirmishers. Following the organizational changes introduced by Childers in 1881, the British light infantry consisted of the following seven regiments (one of which was a Highland unit):

Prince Albert's Light Infantry (Somersetshire Regiment)
The Duke of Cornwall's Light Infantry
The Oxfordshire Light Infantry
The King's Own Light Infantry (South Yorkshire Regiment)
The King's Light Infantry (Shropshire Regiment)
The Durham Light Infantry
The Highland Light Infantry

There were also the Scotch Rifles and Royal Irish Rifles that – despite being designated as 'Rifle' units and being dressed in dark green – had a lot in common with the light infantry regiments. With the general demobilization that followed the Battle of Waterloo, the 60th Regiment of Foot was restructured on just two battalions, which were assigned the dark green uniforms of the disbanded 5th Battalion and were fully re-equipped with rifled carbines (the 2nd Battalion in 1818 and 1st Battalion in 1824). During 1824, the unit assumed the new denomination of the Duke of York's Own Rifle Corps, after King George IV's younger brother; this was changed to the King's Rifle Corps in 1830, when the Duke of York acceded to the throne as William IV. The numeral '60th' was eliminated from the official denomination of the unit only with the British Army's reorganization of 1881. The King's Royal Rifle Corps performed garrison duties for most of the central decades of the nineteenth century. However, after the Crimean War broke out, the British government decided

Rifles and Light Infantry   61

Officer of the King's Royal Rifle Corps wearing an M1878 spiked helmet. (*ASKB*)

to expand the unit by forming a 3rd Battalion in 1855 and a 4th Battalion in 1857. The first three battalions of the corps fought with distinction during the Indian Mutiny. During the 1860s, the special connection with North America of the King's Royal Rifle Corps was renewed when – following the outbreak of the American Civil War – it sent its 4th Battalion to Canada. This was followed, in 1867, by the 1st Battalion, which remained in North America for nine years and participated in the Red River Expedition of 1870 (which was conducted against the Métis rebels). The 2nd Battalion of the King's Royal Rifle Corps participated in the Second Anglo-Afghan War of 1878–80, while detachments of the 3rd and 4th Battalions fought in the Fourth Anglo-Ashanti War. The first three battalions of the King's Royal Rifle Corps all fought with distinction during the Second Boer War.

After the end of the Napoleonic Wars, the 95th Rifle Regiment retained its special status and peculiar methods of training. In 1816, its three battalions received the new official denomination of the Rifle Brigade, and thus the numeral '95th' was eliminated. In 1819, the 3rd Battalion was disbanded as part of the ongoing demobilization of the British Army. Between 1852 and 1861, Prince Albert, the husband of Queen Victoria, was the colonel-in-chief of the Rifle Brigade, which, during this time, became known as the Prince Consort's Own Rifle Brigade (this denomination became official only in 1862, following the death of Prince Albert). The excellent reputation of the unit was preserved by Prince Albert, who paid great attention to its tradition. Both the battalions of the corps took part in the Crimean War, during which they distinguished themselves in several of the bloodiest engagements (the Alma, Inkerman and Sevastopol). Upon the outbreak of hostilities with Russia, the British expanded the Rifle Brigade by forming a 3rd Battalion in 1855 and a 4th Battalion in 1857. The 2nd and 3rd Battalions participated with distinction to the military campaigns of the Indian Mutiny. During the 1860s, the 1st and 4th Battalions were garrisoned in Canada, where they fought against the rebels of the Fenian Brotherhood. The 4th Battalion, in particular, developed a special connection with the North American colony, acting as the guard of both the Governor-General of Canada and the Canadian government from 1862–71. By 1871, most of the British regular units garrisoning Canada had left the country, meaning that the Canadian colonial military had to be completely reorganized in order to replace the British regulars. The 4th Battalion of the Rifle Brigade played an important role in this process, retraining the Canadian militia units for several years. After this, the 4th Battalion took part in the Second Anglo-Afghan War, while the 2nd Battalion participated in the Third Anglo-Ashanti War and the Sudan campaign (1898). The Second Boer War saw the involvement of both the 1st and the 2nd Battalions of the Rifle Brigade. During the period from 1815–1901, the battalions of both the King's Royal Rifle Corps and the Rifle Brigade had the same internal structure as the line infantry units, although with no distinction between centre and flank companies. The only exception to this rule was the temporary expansion to sixteen companies of the two battalions from the Rifle Brigade that took part in the Crimean War.

Uniforms and Equipment

The uniforms worn by both the King's Royal Rifle Corps and the Rifle Brigade were modelled on those of the line infantry, but always had some peculiarities. First of all, they were dark green and not scarlet red; this, together with the use of black belt equipment, resulted in an early form of camouflaging that favoured the skirmishing tactics employed by the British riflemen. Until 1815, the battalions making up the King's Royal Rifle Corps were all dressed like the line infantry, except for the 5th Battalion that was equipped with rifled carbines; when the number of battalions was reduced to two, the whole unit started to be uniformed in dark green and to use black leather equipment. The Rifle Brigade, instead, wore dark green since its foundation in 1800. In 1822, the King's Royal Rifle Corps replaced the dark green uniform used during the Napoleonic Wars with a new one, which comprised a Regency shako and dark green jacket. The headgear had a frontal badge reproducing a Maltese cross, dark green decorative cords and black pompom, while the jacket, being single-breasted and short-skirted, had red facings with black lace (standing collar and pointed cuffs) as well as three rows of buttons on the front (which were connected by black frogging). The outfit was completed by dark green trousers. Officers were dressed quite differently from their men, wearing a hussar-style jacket with full black frogging on the front and black Hungarian knots on the sleeves, as well as a dark green pelisse. The latter, part of the hussars' dress, was a fur-trimmed jacket that was worn on the left shoulder, trimmed with black Astrakhan fur and having black Hungarian knots on the sleeves. In 1824, the black pompom of the shako was replaced with a drooping plume of the same colour; this was quite short-lived, since in 1830 the pompom was reintroduced following the adoption of the new M1828 shako. In 1831, the King's Royal Rifle Corps received a new model of short-tailed jacket, which had three rows of buttons on the front but no black frogging. Like the previous jacket, this was dark green and had red facings as well as black contre-epaulettes. Officers no longer used the pelisse, but still had full black frogging on the front of their jackets. In 1844, the unit adopted the new Albert shako, albeit retaining its distinctive black pompom and frontal plate bearing a Maltese cross. In 1857, the new single-breasted tunic was adopted by the King's Royal Rifle Corps, with red facings piped in black. Following the introduction of the new French-pattern shako, the riflemen adopted all the various models of shako that were introduced for the line infantry but always with black pompom and frontal badge reproducing a bugle horn. After the adoption of the tunic in 1857, the King's Royal Rifle Corps was always dressed in the same tunic used by the line infantry, but in dark green with red facings. In addition, the unit had black piping to collar and cuffs; the latter were pointed and thus had no cuff flaps. Officers continued to present a distinctive appearance, their tunics having black frogging on the front and black Hungarian knots on the sleeves. Trousers remained dark green for all ranks. In 1873, it was decided to replace the shako with a busby, which was thought to be more fitting for riflemen than the previous headgear. The M1873 busby was made of black lambskin for officers and black sealskin for the men, bearing a bugle horn badge on the front together with a black cockade and black plume. In 1878, the standard helmet of the line infantry replaced the busby, but this latter was reissued (albeit with a different shape) in 1891.

The Rifle Brigade was always dressed almost identically to the King's Royal Rifle Corps, but with black facings instead of red. The Regency shako had been adopted by the unit in 1816. The dark green jacket used during the closing phases of the Napoleonic Wars, being single-breasted and having no frontal frogging, remained in use until 1831, when it was replaced with a new short-tailed jacket that was double-

Private (left) and officer (right) of the Rifle Brigade wearing the M1878 spiked helmet. (*ASKB*)

breasted and had no frontal frogging. The new jacket had black contre-epaulettes and cuff flaps. The headgear of the Rifle Brigade, after the adoption of the Regency shako, followed the same evolution as that of the King's Royal Rifle Corps; it should be noted, however, that the latter had gilt fittings (including the frontal plate) while the Rifle Brigade had white metal fittings. The short-lived drooping plume introduced for the Regency shako was dark green rather than black for the Rifle Brigade. In 1831, the Rifle Brigade also received the new model of short-tailed jacket, which had two rows of buttons on the front but no black frogging. Officers no longer used the pelisse, but still had full black frogging on the front of their jackets. In 1857, the new single-breasted tunic was adopted by the Rifle Brigade, with black facings. Thereafter, they were always dressed in the same tunic used by the line infantry, but in dark green with black facings. Officers' tunics had black frogging on the front and

Rifles and Light Infantry 65

Privates of the Scotch Rifles wearing the dark green shako and trews trousers. As an alternative to the shako shown here, the new rifle units created in 1881 could wear the M1878 spiked helmet covered with dark green cloth. (*ASKB*)

black Hungarian knots on the sleeves. Trousers were always dark green for all ranks. The Rifle Brigade received the short-lived M1873 busby before being assigned the M1878 helmet and then the M1891 busby. The Scotch Rifles, created in 1881, were dressed like the Rifle Brigade in dark green with black facings, but had Highland doublets with Inverness flaps instead of the standard tunics and wore trews made of tartan cloth. The Royal Irish Rifles were dressed exactly like the Rifle Brigade, but with dark green facings since they were an Irish unit.

Until 1837, the rifle units of the British infantry were equipped with the excellent Baker rifle, a very accurate muzzle-loading flintlock weapon that was specifically designed for the newly born Rifle Corps and performed extremely well during the Napoleonic Wars. The Baker rifle was replaced with the newly developed Brunswick rifle from 1837, the muzzle-loading percussion rifle's name being derived from the German state of Brunswick since the British experimented with Hanoverian percussion cap technology during the period in which Britain and the German state of Hanover had the same head of state. Following the introduction of the Pattern 1853 Enfield rifle, the Rifle Corps and the line infantry units of the British Army started to be equipped with the same weapons.

Chapter 3

Guard and Heavy Cavalry

History and Organization

Like all the major European military forces of the nineteenth century, the British Army had some cavalry units that had 'Guard' status. These acted as the mounted bodyguard of the royal family and were considered to be the elite of the British heavy cavalry. During the reign of Queen Victoria, there were three British mounted guard corps: 1st Regiment of Life Guards, 2nd Regiment of Life Guards and Royal Horse Guards. The history of the Life Guards began in 1658, when England and Scotland were still two independent realms ruled by the same monarch and they were originally part of the English army. The 1st Troop of Life Guards was raised in 1658 by Charles II during his exile in the Spanish Netherlands, the elite cavalry corps being chosen from his most loyal followers. During the same year, a 2nd Troop of Life Guards was established, with the official denomination of the Duke of York's Troop of Horse Guards. A 3rd Troop of Life Guards was added in 1659, being commonly known as Monck's Lifeguards, acting as the mounted bodyguard of George Monck, the main political supporter of Charles II during his exile. The members of the three Lifeguard units were known as 'gentlemen', all coming from the higher social classes of England and being required to provide their own horses and uniforms. In 1660, with the Stuart Restoration, Charles II returned to England and regained his throne. The Life Guards were thereby absorbed into the reorganized English army and continued to act as the mounted bodyguard of the king. In 1678, one company of horse grenadiers was added to each troop of Life Guards, made up of ordinary soldiers rather than gentlemen. In 1686, a 4th Troop of Life Guard – with an attached company of horse grenadiers – was raised by James II as part of a larger expansion of the English army. In addition to the four units described above, which were all part of the English army, there was also a Scottish corps of Life Guards, which was formed by Viscount Newburgh in 1661 shortly after the Restoration of Charles II. A Scottish 2nd Troop of Life Guards was raised soon after, but this had a very short history, being disbanded in 1676. During James II's reign, Ireland also had an independent Troop of Life Guards, with an attached company of horse grenadiers like the English Life Guards. This was quartered in Dublin and acted as the mounted bodyguard of the king when he was in Ireland.

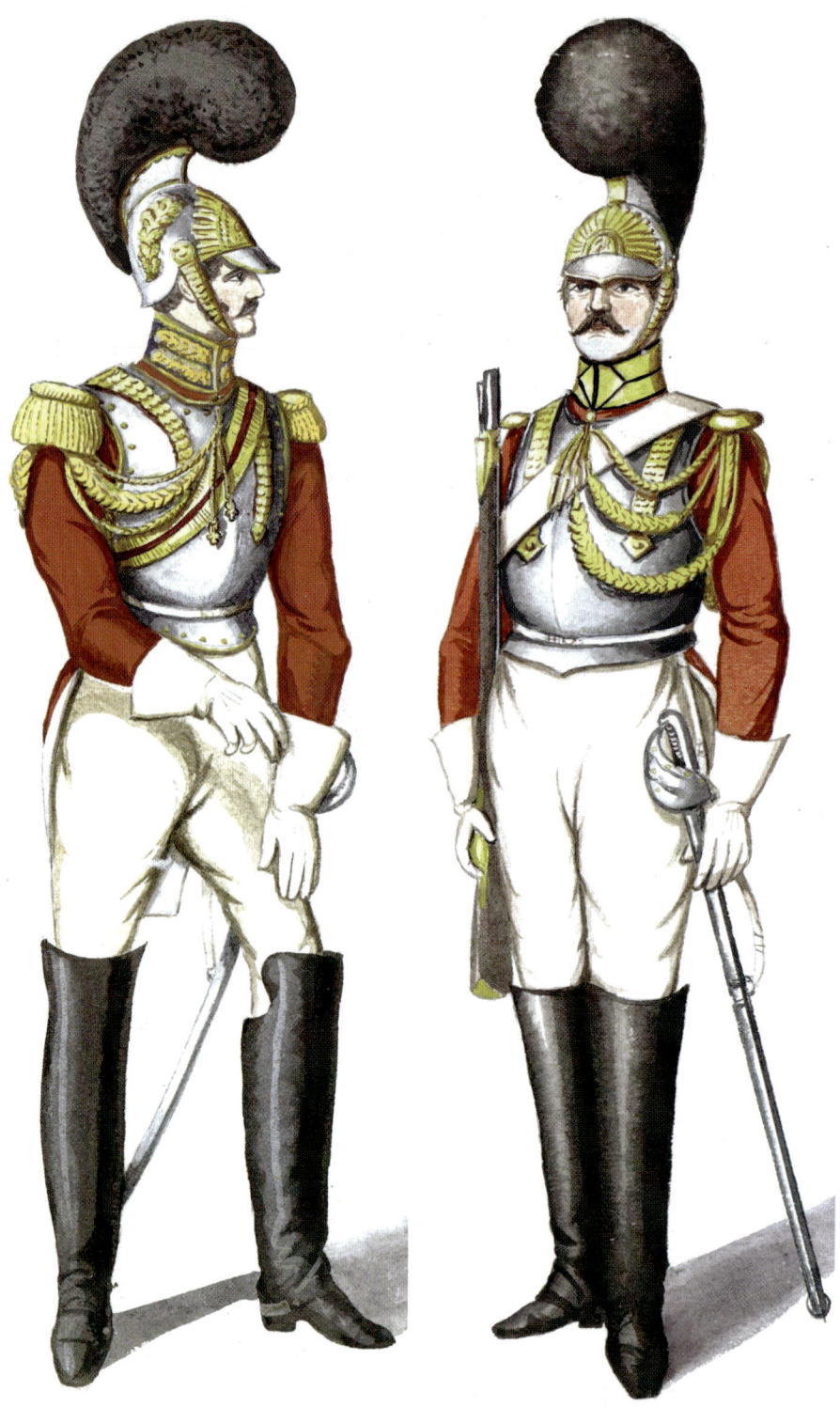

Officer (left) and trooper (right) of the Life Guards wearing the M1817 German helmet.

Guard and Heavy Cavalry 69

Trooper of the Life Guards wearing an M1817 German helmet. (*ASKB*)

With the outbreak of the Glorious Revolution in 1688 and the subsequent landing of William of Orange in England, the internal organization of the Life Guards was changed significantly. The armies of England, Scotland and Ireland remained independent from each other, but the new English king rationalized their internal structures. The English 4th Troop of Life Guards, which had been recently formed by James II, was disbanded in 1689. During the following ten years, it was replaced by a foreign military unit from the Netherlands that was on English pay: the Garde du Corps. William of Orange was also the supreme ruler of the Netherlands, and the invasion force with which he landed in England was mostly made up of Dutch troops. Being unsure of the loyalty of his new subjects, William retained several Dutch units on English pay long after the end of the Glorious Revolution. The soldiers of the Garde du Corps, which had also taken up the title of the 4th Troop of Life Guards, returned to their homeland only in 1699. The Scottish Life Guards remained loyal to James II during the Glorious Revolution and most of them resigned their military positions, but William of Orange soon re-established the unit with new gentlemen who were loyal to his cause. The troop of Irish Life Guards was permanently disbanded, its members following James II into exile and continuing to serve the deposed monarch in France. In 1709, the English

Officer of the Horse Guards wearing an M1817 German helmet. (*ASKB*)

Guard and Heavy Cavalry 71

Trooper of the Horse Guards wearing an M1817 German helmet.

Officer of the Life Guards wearing an M1831 bearskin. (*ASKB*)

and Scottish armies were merged to form the new British Army, as a result of which the Scottish Life Guards were assembled with their English equivalents and became the new 4th Troop of Life Guards.

Meanwhile, in 1693, the three troops of English horse grenadiers had been assembled into a single unit known as the Horse Grenadier Guards. These had the numerical establishment of a single troop but were completely independent from the gentlemen of the Life Guards. In 1702, a troop of horse grenadiers was raised in Scotland and attached to the Scottish Life Guards; when the latter became part of the British Army in 1709, it was detached from its mother corps and became an independent unit. Consequently, the new British Army had a 1st Troop of Horse Grenadiers and a 2nd Troop of Horse Grenadiers, in addition to the four troops of Life Guards. From their foundation, the units of Life Guards had a distinctive heavy cavalry nature which over time was also acquired by the troops of horse grenadiers, who abandoned their use of hand-grenades and became ordinary heavy cavalry units. In 1746, the 3rd and 4th Troops of Life Guards were disbanded following the outbreak of the Jacobite Rebellion that ravaged Scotland. In 1788, as part of the great organizational changes that took place after the British military defeat in the American Revolution, it was decided to assemble the two remaining troops of Life Guards with the two troops of Horse Grenadiers in order to form two consolidated regiments: the 1st Regiment of Life Guards and the 2nd Regiment of Life Guards. The first was formed by assembling together the 1st Troop of Life Guards and the 1st Troop of Horse Grenadiers; the second was created by merging the 2nd Troop of Life Guards and the 2nd Troop of Horse Grenadiers. With this important organizational change, the nature of the Life Guards changed, the two new regiments being mostly made up of ordinary soldiers rather than aristocratic young gentlemen. Both the 1st and 2nd Regiments of Life Guards served with distinction in the Napoleonic Wars, but during the early part of Queen Victoria's reign they were never sent overseas and thus mostly performed police duties in London. Both regiments provided detachments for the formation of a temporary Household Composite Cavalry Regiment during the Egyptian campaign of 1882 and the Second Boer War.

The Royal Horse Guards, commonly known as The Blues because of their distinctive dark blue uniforms, had a completely different history to the two regiments of Life Guards. In 1650, while Oliver Cromwell was at the peak of his power, a heavy cavalry unit known as the Regiment of Cuirassiers was raised by Sir Arthur Haselrig. From the outset, this corps had a distinct elite status and was mostly employed for escort and policing duties, in many respects performing like a type of Gendarmerie. With the Restoration of Charles II, the Regiment of Cuirassiers was transferred to royal service in 1660 and most of its officers (who were still loyal to the Parliamentarist cause) were replaced by new ones whose loyalties were to the Stuarts. The unit initially consisted of just three troops, whose members were mostly wealthy gentlemen, but by the outbreak of the Glorious Revolution it had eight troops and had the new official name of the King's Regiment of Horse. When William of Orange disembarked in England, the members of the regiment abandoned James II and sided with the Dutch pretender to the English throne. During the early decades of the eighteenth century, the unit continued to serve mostly as a police corps, garrisoning several areas of the kingdom and preventing the outbreak of local rebellions. During the second half of the century, however, the King's Regiment of Horse participated and distinguished itself in several campaigns fought by the British Army on the continent. In 1750, the regiment was assigned the new denomination of the Royal Horse Guards, despite not being part of the Royal Household. In 1788, after having spent several years patrolling the countryside of the East Midlands, the Royal Horse Guards were transferred to London as a result of the reorganization of the Life Guards. In 1800, new barracks were built for the regiment at Windsor and the unit started to perform as the mounted bodyguard of the royal family on a permanent basis, although it was only formally assigned the same status as the Life Guards in 1820. The Royal Horse Guards served with distinction during the Napoleonic Wars, but during the early part of Queen Victoria's reign they were never sent overseas and mostly performed policing duties in London. The regiment – like the two units of Life Guards – provided detachments for the formation of a temporary Household Composite Cavalry Regiment for the Egyptian campaign of 1882 and during the Second Boer War. Throughout the reign of Queen Victoria, the three units making up the Household Cavalry always had the same internal organization as the British Army's heavy cavalry regiments.

Officer (left) and troopers (right) of the Life Guards wearing the M1831 bearskin. (*ASKB*)

Guard and Heavy Cavalry 75

Officer of the Horse Guards wearing an M1831 bearskin. (*ASKB*)

Trooper of the Horse Guards wearing an M1831 bearskin. (*ASKB*)

Troopers of the Life Guards in 1850 wearing the Albert helmet. (*ASKB*)

By the end of the Napoleonic Wars, the British heavy cavalry consisted of two distinct categories, the Dragoon Guards and Dragoons. While formally the Dragoon Guards were heavy horsemen and the Dragoons medium horsemen, in practice there was very little difference between them as they were both trained and equipped to act as 'shock' cavalry. The Dragoon Guards were first created in 1746, when the general organization of the British heavy cavalry underwent a radical reform. The first two heavy cavalry units that received the new denomination of Dragoon Guards were the Queen's Own Regiment of Horse and the Earl of Peterborough's Regiment of Horse, which respectively became the 1st Dragoon Guards and 2nd Dragoon Guards. In

Officer of the Life Guards wearing the M1855 tunic and Albert helmet. (*ASKB*)

1747, a third unit, the Earl of Plymouth's Regiment of Horse, was converted into a regiment of Dragoon Guards. This was followed by another four units in 1788, when the British cavalry was again reorganized, meaning that by 1815, the British Army included a total of seven regiments of Dragoon Guards. Since the days of the Restoration (1660), the English cavalry had been made up of horse regiments and dragoon regiments: the former were equipped with cuirasses until the late seventeenth century and consisted of proper heavy cavalry, whereas the latter were originally raised as mounted infantry who were not tasked with conducting frontal charges. Initially, dragoons were introduced into European armies as chosen units of infantrymen who used horses to travel long distances but dismounted to fight. In practice, they consisted of infantrymen with a higher degree of mobility, as emphasized by their personal equipment, which included infantry muskets rather than cavalry carbines. By the first decades of the eighteenth century, the dragoons had gradually lost their original mounted infantry nature and been transformed into regular heavy cavalry. At the same time, the horse regiments discarded their metal cuirasses and started to use lighter personal equipment. As a result of these changes, the tactical differences that distinguished the horse regiments from the dragoon units practically ceased to exist. In 1746, the British government decided to transform the horse regiments into dragoons in order to cut costs and eliminate a tactical differentiation that no longer existed in practice. The heavy mounts of the horse regiments had a considerable cost but produced no real advantages on the battlefield, and the soldiers of the horse regiments were paid much more than those of the dragoon units. With the creation of the new Dragoon Guards, the costly horse regiments were abolished, but their members were permitted to keep alive the glorious traditions of the British heavy cavalry. The term 'Guards' of their official denomination underlined that the units of Dragoon Guards were the elite of the British heavy cavalry, marking a formal difference between them and the normal dragoons. The transformation of the horse regiments into Dragoon Guards was very unpopular among the units affected, since it led to drastic reductions in pay. Furthermore, their new official denomination did not signify the inclusion of the former horse regiments in the Royal Household. In practice, the Dragoon Guards were placed somewhere between the Life Guards/Horse Guards and the normal regiments of dragoons. One of the new units of Dragoon Guards, the 6th Dragoon Guards, always retained some features of the former horse regiments due to its peculiar history. The unit, raised in 1686, was originally named Lord Lumley's Regiment of Horse. At the start of the Glorious Revolution, it joined William of Orange's cause and went to Ireland to fight against the Jacobite forces. In 1692, the corps was renamed the King's Regiment of Carabineers, and under this denomination it took part in all the major continental campaigns fought by the British Army during the eighteenth century. In most European armies, cavalry units defined as 'Carabineers' were extra-heavy corps that continued to wear cuirasses well into the eighteenth century. The King's Regiment of Carabineers was the direct heir of this glorious military tradition and – despite becoming a standard unit of Dragoon Guards – since 1855 had the privilege of wearing a distinctive dark blue uniform (all the other regiments of Dragoon Guards, as we will see, were dressed in scarlet).

By 1815, the British Army had just five of dragoon regiments, several of the dragoon regiments having been transformed into units of light dragoons (see the

Guard and Heavy Cavalry 79

Trooper of the Horse Guards wearing an M1855 tunic and Albert helmet. (*ASKB*)

Uniforms of the Life Guards and the Horse Guards in 1861; the trumpeter on the left is dressed in the royal livery. (*ASKB*)

next chapter for more details). In 1818, another two of the remaining dragoon regiments were converted into light dragoons, meaning that by the beginning of Queen Victoria's reign in 1837, the British Army deployed just three dragoon units: the 1st Dragoons or Royal Dragoons, the 2nd Dragoons or Royal Scots Greys and the 6th Dragoons or Inniskilling Dragoons. The regiments that were transformed into light dragoons kept their numbers, which is why the three surviving units of dragoons were not numbered in progressive order. It should be noted that the 5th Dragoons were disbanded in 1799, having been accused of sedition, with their regimental number left vacant until 1858. Of all the dragoon regiments, the Royal Scots Greys probably had the most peculiar history. The regiment was originally raised in 1678 as three independent troops of dragoons that were part of the Scots army. At that time, Scotland still had an independent army that was mostly used to perform internal police duties. In 1681, another three troops of dragoons were raised and were brought together with the existing ones in order to form a new unit that assumed the denomination of the Royal Regiment of Scots Dragoons. During this early phase of its history, the unit was already mounted on grey horses and thus

Guard and Heavy Cavalry 81

Officer of the Dragoon Guards wearing an M1818 Minerva helmet. The tail-coat is still that worn during the Napoleonic period, with decorative lace on the buttonholes of the front. (*ASKB*)

Officer of the Dragoon Guards wearing an M1818 Minerva helmet and M1818 tail-coat. (*ASKB*)

Officer (left) and trooper (right) of the Dragoon Guards wearing the M1818 Minerva helmet and M1818 tailcoat. (*ASKB*)

Guard and Heavy Cavalry 83

Trooper of the 6th Dragoons wearing an M1818 Minerva helmet and M1818 tail-coat.

received its famous nickname of the Scots Greys. With the outbreak of the Glorious Revolution, like the rest of the Scots army, the Royal Regiment of Scots Dragoons sided with William of Orange and helped him in crushing the revolt of the Scottish Jacobites. After assuming the new name of the Royal North British Dragoons, the corps was absorbed with the rest of the Scots army into the newly formed British Army. The Royal North British Dragoons participated with distinction in all the major continental campaigns fought by the British Army during the second half of the eighteenth century, and in 1768 they were permitted to wear a distinctive bearskin headgear. At the Battle of Waterloo, the regiment charged to the cry of 'Scotland forever!', consolidated its already glorious combat reputation. When Britain became

Officer of the 2nd Dragoons wearing an M1820 bearskin and M1818 tail-coat. (*ASKB*)

involved in the Crimean War, an entire temporary cavalry division was formed to be sent overseas, comprising one brigade of heavy cavalry and one of light cavalry. The Heavy Brigade consisted of all the regiments of dragoons in the British Army: the 4th Regiment of Dragoon Guards, 5th Regiment of Dragoon Guards, 1st Regiment of Dragoons, 2nd Regiment of Dragoons and 6th Regiment of Dragoons. The Heavy Brigade performed very well in several actions during the Crimean War. During Queen Victoria's reign, all the British heavy cavalry regiments – whether Dragoon Guards or Dragoons – had an internal structure of three active squadrons and one depot squadron. A single squadron consisted of two troops; squadrons were known by letters, while troops went by numbers. The single depot squadron was intended

Officer of the Dragoon Guards wearing an M1834 helmet. (*ASKB*)

Officer of the Dragoon Guards wearing an M1843 helmet, which was adopted by the Dragoons from 1842. (*ASKB*)

to provide new recruits with some solid basic training for the three active squadrons, in order to replenish their losses and vacancies. The great organizational reforms of the British Army during the second half of the nineteenth century did not affect the cavalry regiments; the various volunteer units of yeomanry cavalry that existed across Britain, for example, were never attached to the regular units, since the latter did not undergo the 'localization' process in which the infantry regiments were involved.

Officer of the 6th Dragoon Guards (Carabineers) wearing an M1855 jacket and Albert helmet. (*ASKB*)

Uniforms and Equipment

In 1817, the Life Guards received a new uniform that included, like the previous one, a scarlet red single-breasted tail-coat with short tails and dark blue facings decorated with yellow lace. The tail-coat was worn together with white breeches for parade dress and with grey trousers with a red side-stripe for service dress. In 1817, the Life Guards were transformed into two cuirassier regiments and thus, together with the tail-coat described above, received a white metal cuirass and a new model of helmet. The cuirass was worn together with yellow aiguillettes (decorative cords) that were applied on the left shoulder, while the helmet had a distinct German appearance, consisting of a silver skull decorated with gilt fittings, surmounted by a high crest of bearskin. The helmet had gilt chin scales and a frontal plate bearing the coat of arms of Hanover. The decision to transform the Life Guards into cuirassiers was taken after the superior officers of the British Army saw the French cuirassiers of Napoleon in action at the Battle of Waterloo. In 1820, the helmet was replaced with a massive black bearskin, which had a gilt plate on the front. The introduction of the bearskin, which was similar to that worn by the Grenadier Guards, confirmed the new extra-heavy nature that had been assumed by the Life Guards following the adoption of cuirasses in 1817. In 1833, the bearskin was slightly modified, its frontal plate replaced by a gilt flaming grenade and the headgear being surmounted by a white plume. In 1842, a new model of helmet, known as the Albert helmet as it was designed by Prince Albert, was introduced. This replaced both the M1817 helmet – which had continued to be used with service dress – and the bearskin that was worn with parade dress. The Albert helmet soon became very popular, to the point that – despite having been slightly modified over time – it is still worn by the Household cavalry today. The new headgear was clearly inspired by the spiked helmet that was used by the contemporary Prussian heavy cavalry, being silver with gilt fittings and surmounted by a spike, to which a white hair plume was attached. For the 1st Regiment of Life Guards the plume fell normally, while for the 2nd Regiment of Life Guards it was gathered into a ball-shaped 'onion' at the top of the spike before falling. In 1855, the Life Guards replaced their scarlet tail-coats with single-breasted tunics of the same colour, having dark blue facings. These were used together with white breeches and are still worn by the Life Guards today. The Horse Guards have been dressed similarly to the Life Guards since the late eighteenth century. In 1817, they received a new uniform that included, like the previous one, a dark blue single-breasted tail-coat with short tails and red facings decorated with yellow lace. The tail-coat was worn together with white breeches for parade dress, and with dark blue trousers having a red side-stripe for service dress. In 1817, the Horse Guards were

Guard and Heavy Cavalry 89

Officer of the 3rd Dragoon Guards wearing an M1855 tunic and Albert helmet. (*ASKB*)

transformed into a cuirassier regiment and thus, together with the tail-coat described above, received a white metal cuirass and the new M1817 helmet. In 1833, the latter was replaced by the new black bearskin that was already used by the Life Guards; this was surmounted by a red plume for the Horse Guards but had no grenade badge on

Officer of the 4th Dragoon Guards wearing an M1855 tunic and Albert helmet.(*ASKB*)

the front. In 1842, the new Albert helmet was adopted, which had a red hair plume for the Horse Guards. In 1855, they replaced their dark blue tail-coats with single-breasted tunics of the same colour, having red facings. These were used together with white breeches and are still worn by the Horse Guards today.

In 1818, the Dragoon Guards were issued with a new uniform, which included a scarlet single-breasted tail-coat with short tails and facings in regimental colour. The tail-coat had golden epaulettes for officers and brass contre-epaulettes for rankers; on the standing collar and round cuffs it bore golden lace for officers and yellow lace

Officer (left) and trumpeter (right) of the 6th Dragoon Guards (Carabineers) wearing an M1855 tunic and Albert helmet. The tunic was adopted by the Carabineers in 1863. (*ASKB*)

for rankers. The tail-coat was worn with the M1818 helmet, which was also known as a Roman or Minerva helmet since it was clearly inspired by those of Ancient Rome. This had a black japanned skull bearing fire gilt laurel spray decorations and a black japanned comb that was topped by a black bearskin crest. On the front of the headgear was a gilt plate bearing the royal coat of arms and regimental title. Trousers could be dark blue or grey, depending on the unit. In 1834, a new model of helmet was introduced, which was all brass for rankers and gilded metal for officers, surmounted by a black bearskin crest that was easily detachable. The bearskin crest was worn with parade dress, being replaced by a lion-shaped device made of brass or gilded metal with service dress that was applied only when the crest was not worn. In 1843, the costly M1834 helmet was replaced by a simpler one, made of brass for rankers and gilded metal for officers. This had a black tuft on the front and a black horsehair mane, and thus looked similar to French helmets of the Napoleonic period. In 1847, the Dragoon Guards also adopted the Albert helmet, which in their case was gilded for officers and brass for rankers. The colour of the falling plume was black until 1855, when regimental-coloured plumes were authorized. In 1855, the

Officers of the 6th Dragoon Guards (Carabineers) in 1895.
The figure on the right is wearing service dress. (*ASKB*)

scarlet red tail-coats were replaced with single-breasted tunics of the same colour, having facings in regimental colour. These changed very little during the following decades and were worn together with dark blue trousers that had a golden side-stripe. The 6th Dragoon Guards, or Carabineers, had the privilege of being dressed in dark blue from 1855. They were initially assigned a dark blue double-breasted jacket with white facings, which was worn only by rankers, officers being given a tunic-shaped single-breasted jacket (always in dark blue) that had white facings and golden frontal frogging. In 1863, the Carabineers received the same single-breasted tunic that had

Officer of the 4th Dragoon Guards in 1895. (*ASKB*)   Officer of the 6th Dragoons in 1895. (*ASKB*)

Trooper (left) and NCO (right) of the 6th Dragoons in 1895.

Guard and Heavy Cavalry 95

already been issued to the other regiments of Dragoon Guards, but in dark blue with white facings. The headgear of the Carabineers was always the same as that used by the other units of Dragoon Guards.

During Queen Victoria's reign, the regiments of Dragoons were always dressed similarly to those of Dragoon Guards. In 1819, the Dragoons were issued with a new uniform, which included a scarlet tail-coat with facings in regimental colour and yellow loops across the front that made up a plastron, the shape of which tapered from top to bottom. On each sleeve and tail of the tail-coat were three pairs of yellow decorative loops, as opposed to the four pairs on the tail-coat of the Dragoon Guards. The helmet was of the Minerva type, and the outfit was completed by dark blue or grey trousers, depending on the unit. In 1823, the tail-coat with frontal plastron fell out of use and was replaced by the same one worn by the Dragoon Guards, albeit with three pairs of yellow loops on each sleeve instead of the Dragoon Guards' four. In 1842, a new model of helmet was introduced, which was adopted also by the Dragoon Guards during the following year. As previously mentioned, this was made of brass for rankers and of gilded metal for officers, with a black tuft on the front and a black horsehair mane. In 1847, the Dragoons also began to wear the Albert helmet, which in their case was gilded for officers and brass for rankers. The colour of the falling plume was black until 1855, when regimental-coloured plumes were introduced. In 1855, the Albert helmet of the Dragoons became silver for officers and white metal for rankers,

Officer of the 2nd Dragoons in 1895. (*ASKB*)

NCO of the 13th Hussars (left) and NCO of the 2nd Dragoons (right) in 1895. (*ASKB*)

in order to distinguish the Dragoons from the Dragoon Guards. In 1855, the scarlet red tail-coats were replaced with single-breasted tunics of the same colour, having facings in regimental colour. Until 1864, the new tunic continued to have yellow lace loops on the sleeves, being worn with dark blue trousers with yellow side-stripe. The 2nd Dragoons, or Royal Scots Greys, had the privilege of wearing a distinctive black bearskin as headgear from 1768. At the beginning of Queen Victoria's reign, this looked quite similar to the one worn by the Household Cavalry, being surmounted by a white plume and having a gilt frontal plate. Over time, however, it was simplified, the white plume becoming a standing one and the frontal plate being removed.

Until 1853, the Dragoon Guards and the Dragoons were equipped with the M1821 heavy cavalry sword, which had a bowl guard and straight blade. In 1853, a new model of sword came into use, the first universal cut-and-thrust weapon for the British cavalry arm, being used by both the heavy cavalry and the light cavalry. The blade of the M1853 sword was slightly curved and had a tip that was double-edged and spear-pointed. The three-bar hilt of the weapon, however, was susceptible to breaking, so an updated model of the sword was introduced in 1864 that had a bowl-shaped guard but its blade was too blunt for cuts. In 1882, a new cavalry sword came into use, which was produced in two different versions: one with longer blade for the heavy cavalry and the other with shorter blade for the light cavalry. Three years later, a new version of the same weapon was distributed to the mounted regiments, with a heavier blade and reinforced hilt. The M1885 sword had a scabbard that could be fastened to the saddle. The improvement of the M1882 sword continued, and in 1890 a new model of the weapon started to be produced, but this too failed to meet expectations once employed in combat. In 1899, a new cavalry sword was designed, which remained in use until 1908. This had a thick and short blade as well as a plain bowl guard, but despite being undoubtedly robust, it proved to be clumsy and ill-balanced. Regarding firearms, until 1842 the British cavalry was equipped with the Brown Bess flintlock carbine that was extensively used during the Napoleonic Wars. The Brown Bess was replaced by the Pattern 1842 carbine, a percussion-lock conversion of the Brown Bess. The Pattern 1842 carbine was replaced during the Indian Mutiny by the Pattern 1856 Enfield rifled carbine, which was the first rifle weapon used by the British cavalry. During the following decades, the British mounted troops were always equipped with carbine versions of the various rifles adopted by the infantry: the Snider-Enfield (the first breech-loading weapon used by the British cavalry), Martini-Henry, Lee-Metford and Lee-Enfield.

Chapter 4

Light Cavalry

History and Organization

Until 1745, the British Army comprised only heavy cavalry units (horse regiments) and medium cavalry units (dragoon regiments). In that year, however, the Jacobite Rising began in Scotland, during which British mounted troops experienced serious difficulties in chasing the highly mobile insurgent forces of the Highlanders, who moved very rapidly on the broken terrain of their homeland and were masters of hit-and-run tactics. Consequently, the Duke of Kingston, one of the English nobles who supported the British efforts against the Jacobites, decided to raise a volunteer horse regiment having light cavalry training from his lands in Nottinghamshire. This new corps, organized by the duke at his own expense, was officially ranked as the 10th Regiment of Horse of the British Army, but its members were trained as light cavalrymen despite being equipped and uniformed like standard heavy horsemen. The Duke of Kingston's Regiment of Horse performed extremely well during the Jacobite Rising and fought in the decisive Battle of Culloden, after which it pursued the defeated Jacobites with great determination. Initially, the regulars of the British Army strongly opposed this new light corps, but combat experience showed the potential of such a unit. After the end of the Jacobite Rising, in 1746, the experimental volunteer regiment raised by the Duke of Kingston was disbanded, its members having enlisted only for the duration of the war. The Duke of Cumberland, who had commanded the British forces at Culloden, had a very positive opinion of the unit and would have preferred to retain it in service. Although this was not possible for practical reasons, Cumberland found a way to maintain some light cavalry in his forces, organizing a new light cavalry unit known as the Duke of Cumberland's Regiment of Light Dragoons, in which he enlisted all the men of the recently disbanded Duke of Kingston's Regiment of Horse. This was the first regular light cavalry unit in the British Army and the first to be classified as Light Dragoons. The regiment was soon dispatched to continental Europe and took part in the final operations of the War of the Austrian Succession (1740–48). In 1749, the Duke of Cumberland's Regiment of Light Dragoons was disbanded after the end of hostilities in Europe. Cumberland was one of the first British officers

Light Cavalry 99

Officer of the 17th Light Dragoons wearing an M1812 shako and M1812 jacket. (*ASKB*)

to understand the importance and potential of the new light cavalry corps; during the Jacobite Uprising, for example, he had a small personal bodyguard formed by a few hussars who were recruited in Hungary. These, despite being just a few men, fought with distinction at Culloden and made a good impression on the more traditionalist officers of the British Army. These Duke of Cumberland's Hussars were the first unit of the British Army to wear the traditional dress of the Hungarian light cavalry. Following the outbreak of the Seven Years' War, the need for new light cavalry units became increasingly strong in all the major armies of the time, and the British Army was no exception.

In April 1757, the formation of a total of eleven independent troops of light cavalry was authorized, each to be attached to one of the existing horse regiments. Members of these new troops were chosen from the youngest and fittest recruits of the existing horse regiments and were mounted on small and nimble horses, being trained to act as skirmishers and explorers. The new light horsemen continued to wear the standard uniforms of their parent regiments, but received a distinctive headgear: a black leather helmet with an upright comb, a frontal plate mounted with brass and a drooping feather. They were still armed with straight-bladed swords, but also carried a flintlock carbine and a couple of pistols. The glorious tradition of the British Light Dragoons was thus born. Within just a few years, the new light troops showed such potential that in 1759 it was decided to form seven regiments of light cavalry. The late eighteenth century saw the rapid expansion of the British light cavalry arm, with several dragoon regiments being transformed into

Trooper (left) and officer (right) of the 4th Light Dragoons wearing the M1828 shako and M1831 jacket. (*ASKB*)

light dragoons. By 1803, the British Army comprised a total of nineteen regiments of light dragoons, numbered 7–25 (the regiments numbered 1–6 were dragoons).

During the Napoleonic Wars, however, it became apparent that the British light cavalry had to undergo some internal 'tactical differentiation' since all its regiments – despite their official denomination – were usually accustomed to perform as medium cavalry and were not used to skirmish in open order like the French light mounted troops. Napoleon's light cavalry included not only mounted chasseurs – the equivalent of the British light dragoons – but also hussars and lancers. Hussars originated in Hungary as an 'extra-light' kind of cavalry, providing scouts and skirmishers who were capable of conducting rapid incursions thanks to their high level of mobility. The lancers originated in Poland as uhlans, medium cavalry capable of scouting as well as conducting effective frontal charges, utilizing their spears to

NCO of the 14th Light Dragoons wearing an M1840 shako and M1840 jacket. (*ASKB*)

Officers of the 3rd Light Dragoons wearing the M1840 shako and M1840 jacket. The headgear of the figure on the left has the black oilskin cover that was used on campaign. (*ASKB*)

full effect. The hussar and lancer units of the French light cavalry obtained some astonishing victories during the Napoleonic Wars, which convinced the British high command to introduce such units into their own mounted troops by converting some of the existing light dragoon regiments. This was a quite complex process, which began during the Napoleonic Wars for the hussars and after 1815 for the lancers. Indeed, the British faced Napoleon's lancer regiments at Waterloo and were highly impressed by their combat capabilities. After 1815, the British also decided to reduce the number of their dragoon regiments by converting two of them into light dragoons. The progressive tactical transformation of the British light cavalry took place according to the following scheme, in a period that partly coincided with the post-1815 demobilization of the British Army:

3rd Dragoons: transformed into a light dragoon regiment in 1818
4th Dragoons: transformed into a light dragoon regiment in 1818
7th Light Dragoons: transformed into a hussar regiment in 1807
8th Light Dragoons: transformed into a hussar regiment in 1818
9th Light Dragoons: transformed into a lancer regiment in 1816
10th Light Dragoons: transformed into a hussar regiment in 1806
11th Light Dragoons: remained a light dragoon regiment
12th Light Dragoons: transformed into a lancer regiment in 1816
13th Light Dragoons: remained a light dragoon regiment
14th Light Dragoons: remained a light dragoon regiment
15th Light Dragoons: transformed into a hussar regiment in 1807
16th Light Dragoons: transformed into a lancer regiment in 1816
17th Light Dragoons: transformed into a lancer regiment in 1823
18th Light Dragoons: disbanded in 1821
19th Light Dragoons: transformed into a lancer regiment in 1816, disbanded in 1821
20th Light Dragoons: disbanded in 1818
21st Light Dragoons: disbanded in 1819
22nd Light Dragoons: disbanded in 1820
23rd Light Dragoons: disbanded in 1817
24th Light Dragoons: disbanded in 1819
25th Light Dragoons: disbanded in 1819

As a result of the above, by the beginning of Queen Victoria's reign in 1837 the British light cavalry consisted of thirteen units: five regiments of light dragoons, four regiments of hussars and four regiments of lancers. The formation of the hussar and lancer units transformed the light cavalry of the British Army into a colourful branch-of-service, the hussars wearing flamboyant uniforms in the Hungarian style while the lancers were dressed in elegant Polish-style uniforms. Retraining former light dragoons as lancers was not an easy task, the spear never having been a traditional weapon of the British cavalry, but by the 1830s, the general quality of the lancer regiments was already excellent. When Britain became involved in the Crimean War, the Light Brigade consisted of the 4th Light Dragoons, 8th Hussars, 11th Light Dragoons, 13th Light Dragoons and 17th Lancers. The Light Brigade was the protagonist of the most iconic combat action of the Crimean War, the Charge of the Light Brigade, or 'Charge of the 600', that took place on 25 October 1854 during the Battle of Balaclava. This saw the brave British light cavalrymen launch a foolhardy frontal attack against well-fortified Russian field batteries, a suicide action which was

Trooper of the 11th Light Dragoons wearing an Albert shako and M1856 tunic. (*ASKB*)

Light Cavalry 105

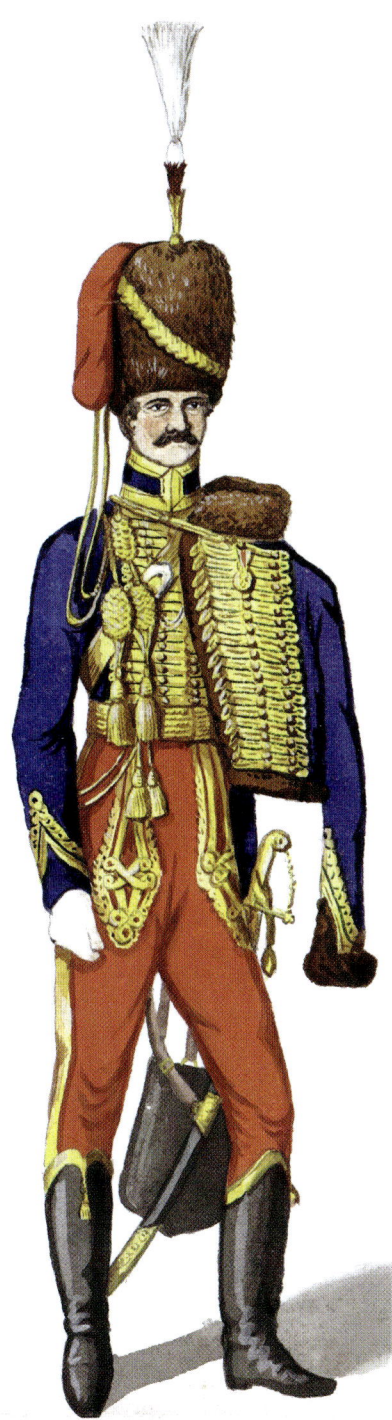

Officer of the 10th Hussars in 1820. The headgear is still the busby worn during the latter years of the Napoleonic Wars.

Officer of the 15th Hussars in 1820. The headgear is the broad-topped shako that was used until 1828. (*ASKB*)

Officer of the 7th Hussars in 1830. The headgear is the new M1828 shako, which still has a standing plume on the front instead of the black falling one. (*ASKB*)

Light Cavalry 107

Trooper of the 7th Hussars in 1830 wearing an M1828 shako.

Officer of the 10th Hussars in 1832 wearing the red pelisse introduced in 1831. (*ASKB*)

the result of a misunderstanding in communication of orders. The Light Brigade, after advancing across what became known as the 'Valley of Death', was able to capture the Russian guns in their entrenched positions. However, the exhausted and wounded British troopers were soon forced to retreat after the Russians mounted a counter-attack with their Cossacks. At the end of the action, 278 British cavalrymen had been killed, wounded or captured. French officer Pierre Bosquet, who took part

Officer of the 10th Hussars in 1848 wearing the new busby that replaced the shako. (*ASKB*)

Trumpeter of the 11th Hussars from the Crimean War.

in the charge, described it as follows: 'It is magnificent, but it is not war. It is madness.' In 1858, following the outbreak of the Indian Mutiny, the 18th Light Dragoons was re-formed and a new lancer regiment was raised, taking the numeral (the 5th) of the dragoon regiment that had been disbanded in 1799 for sedition.

During the Indian Mutiny of 1857–58, most of the cavalry units that were serving with the East India Company rebelled against the British. The company's cavalry had been entirely made up of locally recruited regiments, and thus, when the uprising

Officer of the 11th Hussars wearing an M1856 tunic. (*ASKB*)

started, the authorities found themselves without any European cavalry unit on which to count. In order to face the mounted troops of the mutinied sepoys, the East India Company had no choice but to assemble – quite hastily – four new cavalry regiments that were raised from the European residents in Bengal. These performed quite well during the Indian Mutiny, so when the East India Company was dissolved and India was annexed to the British Empire, it was decided to absorb three of the four units into the British Army (as happened for the company's European infantry). The 1st Bengal European Light Cavalry became the new 19th Hussars, the 2nd Bengal European Light Cavalry became the 20th Hussars, the 3rd Bengal European Light Cavalry became the 21st Hussars and the 4th Bengal European Light Cavalry was disbanded. In 1862, after the absorption of these units was completed, the British authorities decided to eliminate the light dragoon units by converting them into hussar regiments; the tactical differences originally existing between light dragoons and hussars having completely disappeared over time, the only differentiation between

Officers of the 20th Hussars in 1890. (*ASKB*)

the two cavalry types being their uniform. As a result, the following transformations took place: the 3rd Light Dragoons became the 3rd Hussars, the 4th Light Dragoons became the 4th Hussars, the 11th Light Dragoons was now the 11th Hussars, the 13th Light Dragoons was transformed into the 13th Hussars, the 14th Light Dragoons became the 14th Hussars and the 18th Light Dragoons was turned into the 18th Hussars. The decades following 1862 saw no major organizational changes for the British light cavalry, except for the transformation in 1897 of the 21st Hussars into a lancer regiment (the 21st Lancers). Therefore, by 1901, the British light cavalry deployed the following corps (twelve regiments of hussars and six of lancers):

3rd Hussars (The King's Own)
4th Hussars (The Queen's Own)
5th Lancers (Royal Irish Lancers)
7th Hussars (The Queen's Own)
8th Hussars (King's Royal Irish Hussars)
9th Lancers (Queen's Royal Lancers)
10th Hussars (Prince of Wales's Own)
11th Hussars (Prince Albert's Own)
12th Lancers (Prince of Wales's Own)
13th Hussars
14th Hussars (The King's Hussars)
15th Hussars (The King's Hussars)
16th Lancers (The Queen's Lancers)
17th Lancers (The Duke of Cambridge's Own)
18th Hussars
19th Hussars
20th Hussars
21st Lancers

Officer of the 11th Hussars in 1890. (*ASKB*)

During Queen Victoria's reign, all the British light cavalry regiments had an internal structure of three active squadrons and one depot squadron. Each squadron consisted of two troops; squadrons were known by letters, but troops by numbers. The single depot squadron had to provide new recruits with some solid basic training for the three active squadrons, to replenish their losses and vacancies. The British Army's great organizational reforms during the second half of the nineteenth century did not affect the cavalry regiments; the various volunteer units of yeomanry cavalry across Britain, for example, were never attached to the regular units because they did not undergo the localization process that involved the infantry regiments.

Uniforms and Equipment

Until the accession to the throne of William IV, the Light Dragoons continued to wear the uniform that they had used during the Napoleonic Wars. This consisted of a dark blue short-tailed jacket, having facings (standing collar and pointed cuffs) as well as frontal plastron in regimental colour. The jacket had white or yellow epaulettes, depending on the regiment, and was worn with light blue trousers that had a double side-stripe in regimental colour. The headgear was a black French-style shako that had been introduced in 1812; this had a top and bottom band in white or yellow, white or yellow metal chin scales and metal frontal plate, and white falling plume that was painted red at the end. In 1828, the bell-topped shako of the infantry came into use. William IV wanted to dress his whole army in scarlet and thus, in 1831, the Light Dragoons were assigned a brand new uniform that comprised a double-breasted and short-tailed red jacket. This had standing collar and pointed cuffs in regimental colour with yellow piping, as well as golden epaulettes for officers and brass contre-epaulettes for rankers. The jacket was worn together with dark blue trousers having a double side-stripe in regimental colour. The headgear had a white falling plume, brass frontal plate reproducing a Maltese cross placed under a crown, yellow top band and yellow decorative cords. In 1840, following the accession to the throne of Queen Victoria, the shako of the Light Dragoons was slightly modified, becoming more cylindrical in shape, while the double-breasted, short-tailed jacket became dark blue. The jacket had standing collar and pointed cuffs in regimental colour with yellow piping, as well as golden epaulettes for officers and brass contre-epaulettes for rankers. Like the infantry, the Light Dragoons adopted the new Albert shako when it was introduced in the British Army. The new headgear retained the frontal plate and falling plume that were worn on the previous model of shako. In 1856, shortly before their dissolution, the Light Dragoons were issued with hussar-style dark blue single-breasted tunics with standing collar and pointed cuffs in

Light Cavalry 115

Officer of the 9th Lancers in 1825. (*ASKB*)

Trooper (left) and officer (right) of the 9th Lancers in 1825. The trooper is already wearing the new light blue-grey trousers with a side-stripe in regimental colour. (*ASKB*)

regimental colour, yellow piping to the collar, yellow Hungarian knots on the sleeves, yellow frontal frogging and yellow shoulder boards. The new tunic was worn with dark blue trousers that had a yellow double side-stripe. Like the infantry, the Light Dragoons replaced their Albert shako with the new French-style one, but retained their brass Maltese cross and falling plume.

From 1819, the British hussars were dressed in broad-topped shako, dark blue dolman, dark blue pelisse and trousers in regimental colour. The shako, whose shape was similar to that of the Regency version used by the infantry, was black or in the distinctive colour of each regiment. It had a black visor with brass external edging, brass chin scales, yellow decorative cords and yellow top band consisting of interlocking

Officer of the 17th Lancers wearing an M1831 jacket. (*ASKB*)

Officer of the 16th Lancers wearing an M1831 jacket. (*ASKB*)

Light Cavalry 119

Officer of the 9th Lancers wearing an M1840 jacket. (*ASKB*)

Officer of the 12th Lancers wearing an M1840 jacket.

Officer of the 9th Lancers wearing an M1840 jacket. The czapka has the black oilskin cover that was used on campaign.

rings. For some time, the busby made of brown fur that had been issued during the Napoleonic Wars remained in use, but during the 1820s this was substituted by the shako in all regiments. Initially, the broad-topped shako had a standing plume on the front, but this was later replaced with a black falling plume when the headgear was shortened in 1828. The dark blue dolman had no coloured facings, but did have Hungarian knots on the sleeves and rich frontal frogging, while the dark blue pelisse was edged with black fur and was usually worn on the left shoulder. The trousers had a broad side-stripe in the same colour as the jacket's frogging, which was white or yellow depending on the regiment. William IV also tried to redress his hussars in scarlet, as he did the Light Dragoons, but this proved impossible. In 1831, however, the hussars' uniform was slightly modified: the pelisse became red and the trousers dark blue. Early in the reign of Queen Victoria, the colour of the pelisse reverted to dark blue and the shako was replaced with a brown busby that had yellow cords, red side-bag and short white over red standing plume. In 1856, the dress of the British hussars underwent a revolution: the costly and impractical pelisse was abolished and the dolman was replaced with a dark blue single-breasted hussar-style tunic with standing collar and pointed cuffs in dark blue, yellow piping to the collar, yellow Hungarian knots on the sleeves, yellow frontal frogging and yellow shoulder boards. The new tunic was worn with dark blue trousers with a yellow double side-stripe. Only the 11th Hussars – nicknamed the Cherry Pickers – had the

Officers of the 12th Lancers; the figures on the left are wearing service dress, while that on the right is wearing an M1856 tunic with coloured frontal lapels. (*ASKB*)

privilege of wearing crimson trousers instead of the usual dark blue. During the later years of Victoria's reign, the uniform of the British hussars changed very little; the only real innovation was the introduction of regimental-coloured plumes for the busbies, due to the fact that from 1856 all the hussar regiments wore dark blue tunics without coloured facings and dark blue trousers.

The new lancer regiments of the British Army formed after 1816 were dressed in Polish-style, with czapka headgear and kurtka tunic. The czapka was a square-topped cap that had a black leather base stiffened with cane and a cloth top in regimental colour. It also had a black leather peak with brass external edging, brass chin scales, brass frontal plate and white-and-red flowing plume. The kurtka was dark blue with standing collar, pointed cuffs and frontal plastron in regimental colour; it had golden epaulettes for officers and brass contre-epaulettes for rankers. Initially, the uniform of the British lancers was completed by trousers in regimental colour with golden

Officers of the 5th Lancers; the figure on the right is wearing service dress, while that on the left is wearing an M1878 tunic with coloured frontal plastron. (*ASKB*)

side-stripe, but these were later replaced by light blue-grey trousers with side-stripe in regimental colour. In 1831, as ordered by William IV, the lancer regiments were all redressed in scarlet. The czapka remained practically the same, but its flowing plume started to be black for all regiments. The kurtka was replaced by a red double-breasted jacket (very similar to that of the Light Dragoons) that had standing collar and round cuffs in regimental colour with yellow piping, as well as golden epaulettes

Light Cavalry 123

Officers of the 16th Lancers; the figure on the left is wearing service dress, while that on the right is wearing an M1878 tunic with coloured frontal plastron. (*ASKB*)

for officers and brass contre-epaulettes for rankers. The cuffs, differently from those of the Light Dragoons, had red flaps. The jacket was worn with dark blue trousers having a double side-stripe in red (in gold for parade dress). In 1840, with the accession to the throne of Queen Victoria, the jackets of the lancers started to be dark blue with facings in regimental colour; only the 16th Lancers were assigned the privilege of continuing to wear red jackets, since they were the Queen's Lancers. In 1856, the double-breasted jacket was abolished and replaced by a tunic that had standing collar, pointed cuffs and frontal lapels in regimental colour. When buttoned over, the frontal lapels showed their reverse side, which was entirely dark blue. In 1878, they were replaced by a single frontal plastron. The czapka was only modified

Trooper of the 9th Lancers wearing an M1878 tunic, with the frontal plastron showing the dark blue internal side. (*ASKB*)

Officer of the 17th Lancers in 1895. (*ASKB*)

by having its plume in different colours, depending on the regiment. Trousers were dark blue with a double side-stripe in regimental colour.

Until 1853, the Light Dragoons, Hussars and Lancers were equipped with the M1821 light cavalry sword, which had a two-bar hilt and curved blade. With the introduction of the M1853 cavalry sword, the light cavalrymen started to use the same weapons as the heavy cavalry (see previous chapters for more details). The M1816 lance of the early British lancers was quite impracticable as it was 4.87m long, and was replaced in 1820 by a new one with a length of just 2.75m. The M1820 lance had a steel ball at the base of the point, in order to prevent over-penetration and to make withdrawal easier. In 1840, however, a new model of lance started to be produced and this did not have the steel ball. The new lance was improved in 1868 – when the head became triangle-shaped – and was replaced in 1894 when a new model of lance was introduced. Until 1885, shafts were made of bamboo, which was replaced by ash (treated with linseed oil and tar) during the closing years of the century. Regarding firearms, those of the light cavalry were always the same as those used by the heavy cavalry (see previous chapter for further details).

Chapter 5

Artillery and Technical Corps

History and Organization

Until 1716, with the creation of the Royal Artillery, the British Army had no permanent company or battery of artillery: temporary artillery trains were organized by the Ordnance Department only when needed and were usually disbanded at the end of each campaign. In time of peace, several dozen professional gunners served with the Ordnance Department, scattered across Britain and manning the guns of various garrisons. In wartime, they were assembled to form a train and were supplemented with a number of civilian workers and pioneers, the latter being semi-skilled civilian labourers who were contracted only for the duration of a campaign. The drivers of the carts that were used to move the artillery pieces were also civilians. The eighteenth century was a period of great change and progressive professionalization for the British artillery and the smaller technical corps that supported it. The first two permanent companies/batteries of artillery of the British Army were established in 1716 and structured for the first time as independent corps. In 1720, they received the official denomination of Royal Artillery, but in practice they were an autonomous force from their creation. The two original companies were soon increased to four and were assembled – at least from an administrative point of view – with the artillery companies that had been part of the garrisons in Gibraltar and Menorca for several years. As a result of these organizational changes, the Royal Regiment of Artillery was created in 1722. This had the numerical consistency of a battalion, its members quickly becoming famed for their professionalism. From the outset, selection and promotion in the Royal Artillery were based on merit, which resulted in a highly skilled officer corps of this new branch of service. In 1741, to improve the overall quality of all the artillerymen serving across the British Empire, a cadet company was formed at the Royal Military Academy at Woolwich, tasked with training not only the officers of the Royal Artillery Regiment but also those artillery officers who served with the East India Company. In 1757, the Royal Artillery Regiment was reorganized on two battalions with twelve companies each, and its expansion continued during the following decades. By 1780, it comprised four active battalions with eight companies each, two invalid companies employed to perform garrison duties and a military band.

Officer (left) and private (right) of the Royal Artillery wearing the M1828 shako and M1831 tail-coat, together with white summer trousers.

Artillery and Technical Corps 129

Private of the Royal Artillery wearing an M1828 shako and M1831 tail-coat. (*ASKB*)

Officer (left) and private (right) of the Royal Artillery wearing the Albert shako and M1831 tail-coat.

Artillery and Technical Corps 131

Officer of the Royal Artillery wearing a busby and M1855 tunic. (*ASKB*)

By 1803, the foot component of the Royal Artillery consisted of eight battalions, each with ten companies or batteries. A 9th Battalion was raised in 1806, followed by a 10th Battalion in 1808. The various battalions were not employed in the field as complete units, their companies/batteries usually being deployed as autonomous corps. When this happened, they were commonly known as brigades, despite consisting of companies with just six pieces each. Attached to each brigade was a detachment of artillery drivers, tasked with moving the guns in the field. After the Napoleonic Wars, the expansion of the Royal Artillery Regiment continued with the formation of another two foot battalions (the 11th and 12th Battalion) in 1848, so by the time of the Crimean War there were twelve autonomous battalions. Each of these was still structured on eight companies or batteries. A single battery consisted of five guns and one howitzer. These were moved along with their limbers and various wagons that were essential for their employment: eight ammunition wagons, three baggage wagons and one spare-wheel wagon. In addition, each artillery company/battery had a field forge for the repair of damaged pieces. In 1855, the Ordnance Department – which controlled both the Royal Artillery and the other technical corps – was abolished and the administration of its various branches was transferred to the British Army. On 1 July 1859, the foot component of the Royal Artillery was reorganized on brigades, which had eight companies or batteries each like the previous battalions and could be either field brigades or garrison brigades. The six field brigades consisted of foot batteries equipped with field guns, while the eight garrison brigades comprised static batteries tasked with performing garrison duties. A ninth garrison brigade was soon added.

In 1861, following the dissolution of the East India Company, its artillery units – comprising fifty-two foot batteries and twenty-one horse batteries – were absorbed into the Royal Artillery. Consequently, the Royal Artillery's foot component was increased to comprise a total of twelve field brigades and thirteen garrison brigades. The ten new brigades that were formed in 1861, however, were smaller than the existing ones, each having a minimum of four and a maximum of six batteries. As a result of these organizational changes, by 1862 the British foot artillery had a total of 164 companies/batteries (sixty-nine of field artillery and ninety-five of garrison artillery). The new 24th and 25th Brigades, which were both of garrison artillery, were quite short-lived, being disbanded in order to give a standard internal establishment to all the new foot artillery brigades that had been created in 1861. From the 1850s, the British high command tried to improve the quality of the militia artillery units and volunteer artillery corps in Britain, and despite remaining separate from the Royal Artillery, they were increasingly integrated with the British Army in the hope that they could eventually replace the regular artillery in performing static garrison duties.

In 1882, as part of the Childers Reforms, the eleven brigades of garrison artillery were reorganized as eleven territorial divisions of garrison artillery, attached to each of which were the units of militia and volunteer artillery that existed on the territory of each division. The garrison artillery of the British Army thus also underwent the so-called localization scheme. In 1889, the eleven territorial divisions of garrison artillery were amalgamated into three larger divisions: the Eastern Division with headquarters at Dover, the Western Division with headquarters at Plymouth and the Southern Division with headquarters at Portsmouth. At the same time, the first independent units of mountain artillery were created within the metropolitan Royal Artillery. Prior to this, there had never been mountain batteries deployed in Britain, only ten mountain artillery batteries that were part of the British colonial forces in India. In 1889, a division of mountain artillery was created within the garrison

Officers of the Royal Artillery; the figure on the left is wearing service dress, while that on the right is wearing a busby and M1855 tunic. (*ASKB*)

artillery, which consisted of ten batteries. In 1899, the Royal Artillery was divided into three distinct branches of service: Royal Field Artillery, Royal Horse Artillery and Royal Garrison Artillery. The latter continued to be structured on three large territorial divisions plus one mountain artillery division. The Royal Field Artillery, instead, consisted of the field artillery brigades and was responsible for operating medium-calibre guns as well as howitzers. From a formal point of view, the Royal Field Artillery also comprised the ten mountain batteries that were part of the British forces in India. Following the reorganization of 1899–1900, the field artillery of the British Army deployed a total of twenty-eight brigades, each of which had three batteries.

The British Army was quite slow in forming its first units of horse artillery, two troops of this new branch being organized only in January 1793. The horse artillery was equipped with horse-drawn guns of small calibre, its main tactical task being to provide support fire for mounted units. Differently from those of the foot artillery,

NCO of the Royal Horse Artillery (left), private of the Royal Artillery (centre) and NCO of the Royal Artillery (right). The horse artilleryman has a busby and M1855 dolman, while the foot artillerymen have a busby and M1855 tunic. (*ASKB*)

Artillery and Technical Corps 135

Privates of the Royal Artillery in 1875; the figure on the left is wearing service dress. (*ASKB*)

Officer of the Royal Artillery wearing an M1878 spiked helmet. (*ASKB*)

the batteries of the horse artillery were known as troops rather than companies. The internal organization of the new mounted batteries always remained quite similar to that of the cavalry troops, and this was also apparent in the uniforms worn by the horse artillerymen, which were of clear 'light cavalry' cut. Another two troops of horse artillery were formed in November 1793, and by 1801 the number of horse batteries in the British Army had been increased to seven. During the Napoleonic Wars, the number of mounted batteries reached a maximum of twelve, but at the end of hostilities these were reduced to eight. This number was expanded to ten during the Crimean War. The gunners of these units were mounted on horses when their batteries were moved, while the drivers sat on the carriages or limbers of the guns. Each horse battery was equipped with five light guns and one howitzer. The horse artillery of the British Army was also responsible for operating rockets. In 1859, the ten troops or batteries of the horse artillery were assembled together in order to form the Horse Brigade.

In 1861, following the dissolution of the East India Company, its mounted artillery units – consisting of twenty-one batteries – were absorbed into the Royal Artillery. As a result, the horse artillery component was restructured on four brigades; the first of these – the former Horse Brigade – mustered ten troops, while the other four each had from a minimum of four to a maximum of seven troops. On 13 April 1864, the former Horse Brigade was split and created two smaller brigades: A Horse Brigade and B Horse Brigade. At the same time, the four new brigades created in 1861 were renamed as C Horse Brigade, D Horse Brigade, E Horse Brigade and F Horse Brigade. Under the reorganization of 1864, each of the mounted artillery brigades consisted of six batteries. On 14 April 1877, the number of horse artillery brigades was reduced to three, but each of them had a larger internal establishment with ten batteries. In 1882, the horse artillery was restructured on just two brigades, each having thirteen batteries. The brigade system was abandoned in 1889, when the British horse artillery consisted of twenty-six independent batteries designated in a single alphabetical sequence (in order of seniority according to the date of formation). In 1901, the brigade system was revived and the Royal Horse Artillery was reorganized on thirteen small brigades, each having just two batteries.

The Corps of Royal Engineers was set up as a permanent military unit only in 1716. Until then, the British Army had only a few independent officers with specific engineering skills. The formation of an independent Corps of Engineers (the 'Royal' prefix was added in 1787), however, did not change the existing situation in any significant way. Indeed, until the outbreak of the Napoleonic Wars, the Corps of Engineers continued to comprise just a few commissioned officers who had undergone specific technical training. In 1792 there were seventy-three of them, a number that was progressively augmented so that by 1813 the Corps of Royal Engineers mustered a total of 262 officers. They received higher pay when serving overseas and were consulted only when needed, for example to conduct siege operations or to build military infrastructures. This situation did not change between 1815 and 1854, meaning that by the outbreak of the Crimean War, the Royal Engineers were still a corps of specialist officers. The labour force for the Royal Engineers was provided by the Royal Sappers and Miners, a small technical corps originally consisting of twelve companies of military workers that was organized along modern lines by Wellington in 1812. The Royal Sappers and Miners performed a series of auxiliary tasks that were fundamental to the effectiveness of a campaign, which included building and carpentry. From 1812, the soldiers of the Royal Sappers and Miners were commanded by the commissioned officers of the Royal Engineers. In addition to the Royal Engineers and the Royal Sappers and Miners, the British Army of the early nineteenth century also comprised another technical corps: the Royal Staff Corps. This was established in 1798 and provided engineer service under the direct control of the British Army's commander-in-chief. In practice, differently from the Royal Engineers and the Royal Sappers and Miners – who were scattered in small detachments across the British Empire – the Royal Staff Corps acted as the unified engineer force of the British Army's General Staff. Initially, it consisted of just four companies, but it was later expanded to become a battalion. Finding its services no longer needed, the Royal Staff Corps was disbanded in 1837. From 1824–49, the Royal Sappers and Miners were progressively expanded, eventually having a total of twenty-two companies, four of which were specifically tasked with conducting cartographic surveys. The Royal Sappers and Miners, like the Royal Engineers commanding them, had detachments in every corner of the British Empire and were often tasked with the construction of important civilian infrastructures. During the Crimean War, the number of their companies was increased to twenty-six.

In 1855, following the abolition of the Ordnance Department, the Royal Engineers and the Royal Sappers and Miners were assembled together into a single Corps of Royal Engineers, its administration being transferred to the British Army. The new corps was initially structured on twenty-eight companies, which was augmented to thirty-six during the Indian Mutiny. After the end of the Mutiny, the Corps of Royal Engineers was restructured on thirty-four active companies and four depot companies after having absorbed the engineers and sappers who had served under the East India Company. During the latter years of Queen Victoria's reign, the Corps of Royal Engineers continued to be enlarged and its companies started to be distinguished according to their technical specialization. As a result, by the end of the nineteenth century, the British Army had fifty-one companies of engineers, which had a wide range of specializations: nine field companies tasked with supporting the various fighting units, thirteen fortress companies that manned military fortifications and infrastructures, four survey companies, two telegraph companies, two railway companies, nine submarine mining companies and twelve depot companies.

Officer of the Royal Horse Artillery wearing an M1827 bell-shaped shako. (*ASKB*)

NCO of the Royal Horse Artillery wearing an M1827 bell-shaped shako. (*ASKB*)

In 1793, the British Army decided to militarize its artillery drivers, who had previously been unreliable civilian contractors with no discipline and training to speak of. As a result, the new Corps of Royal Artillery Drivers was formed, comprising not only soldiers but also the draught animals and wagons needed to transport artillery guns and materials. By 1808, the Corps of Royal Artillery Drivers, whose members were dressed similarly to the soldiers of the horse artillery, comprised a total of eight troops. Each of these troops deployed 450 drivers organized into five sections of ninety men, 104 assorted craftsmen, 945 draught horses and seventy-five riding horses. By the end of the Napoleonic Wars, the Corps of Royal Artillery Drivers had been expanded to eleven troops, for a total of eighty-eight officers and 7,352 other ranks. Wellington was never particularly happy with his Corps of Royal Artillery Drivers, its members sometimes lacking discipline and not being commanded by competent officers. As a result, in 1817, the corps was temporarily absorbed into the Royal Artillery before being disbanded in 1822. In addition to the Corps of Royal Artillery Drivers, the British Army of the early nineteenth century also included the Royal Waggon Train, which was tasked with transporting all those materials of the army that did not belong to the artillery. This was established in 1798 – mostly with men drafted from the cavalry – and initially consisted of just three troops. During the Napoleonic Wars, the Royal

Officer of the Royal Horse Artillery wearing an M1837 busby.

Officer of the Royal Horse Artillery wearing an M1855 dolman.

Waggon Train was progressively expanded, and by 1814 it was structured on fourteen troops with a total of around 1,900 men. Generally speaking, like their equivalents of the Royal Artillery, the drivers of the Royal Waggon Train were not well known for their discipline or efficiency. In 1818, the corps was reduced to just two troops, and was completely disbanded in 1833. As a consequence, when the Crimean War broke out, the British Army had no train units that could transport its materials on campaign. This caused serious problems during the early stages of the fighting against the Russians, to the point that in January 1855 it was decided to form a new Land

Officer of the Royal Horse Artillery in 1890. (*ASKB*)

Officer of the Royal Horse Artillery in 1895. (*ASKB*)

Trooper of the Royal Horse Artillery in 1895. (*ASKB*)

Artillery and Technical Corps 145

NCO of the Royal Sappers and Miners wearing an M1828 shako and M1831 tail-coat. (*ASKB*)

Transport Corps. Becoming known as the Military Train in 1856, it consisted of seven battalions. In 1869, the Commissariat (a civilian body responsible for providing food and forage to the army) and the Store Department (a civilian body that provided the army with weapons and ammunition) were merged with the Military Train to form the new Army Service Corps. By 1871, this new body comprised twelve transport companies as well as seven supply companies (the former Commissariat) and three ordnance companies (the former Store Department). In 1881, the Army Service Corps was split to form two distinct units: the Commissariat and Transport Corps (made up of the transport and supply companies) and the Ordnance Corps (comprising the ordnance companies). In 1888, these two new units were again merged together and the Army Service Corps was re-formed.

Among the minor formations of the British Army during the nineteenth century were those units that later gave birth to the Military Police. During the Napoleonic Wars, Wellington created a small mounted unit known as the Staff Corps of Cavalry, which was tasked with keeping law and order within the British Army when it was on campaign. Following the outbreak of the Crimean War, the British decided to create another temporary unit of military police that was quite similar to that formed by Wellington: the Mounted Staff Corps, which consisted of fifty policemen who were mostly recruited from the Irish Constabulary. This was a provost corps tasked with enforcing discipline among British soldiers who operated overseas, preventing desertion and looting but also performing other auxiliary duties. They received extra pay for their service and wore a distinctive uniform. The Mounted Staff Corps, however, did not perform particularly well and was disbanded in the autumn of 1855. Some months later, a new attempt to organize a military police force was made by the British, a total of twenty-one NCOs and troopers, from different cavalry units, forming the Military Mounted Police Corps. This unit was more success and was slowly expanded during the following decades, officially becoming a permanent unit in 1877, when its establishment was fixed at seventy-five men. In 1882, a sister corps to the Military Mounted Police – the Military Foot Police – was formed, becoming a permanent unit in 1885, when it comprised ninety men. By the end of Queen Victoria's reign, the two corps of military police of the British Army mustered around 300 men, who were scattered across the British Empire.

Uniforms and Equipment

From its creation, the Royal Artillery was always dressed similarly to the line infantry, but in dark blue with red facings. Until 1831, the foot artillerymen wore a dark blue single-breasted tail-coat that had red facings (standing collar and round cuffs), yellow piping to the collar, yellow flaming grenade badge on the collar, red shoulder straps piped in yellow and yellow pointed lace loops on the buttonholes of the front and the cuffs. The tail-coat was worn with sky blue-grey trousers during cold months and with white ones during hot months. The headgear was a Regency shako with brass frontal plate and white plume, which was replaced by the new M1828 shako. In 1831, a new model of tail-coat was introduced, with two close rows of buttons down the front and cuff flaps with three buttons each. The cuff flaps were red and their buttonholes were laced in yellow, but the buttons on the front of the tail-coat had no yellow lace on the buttonholes. The collar had decorative yellow lace. On the M1831 tail-coat, the previous shoulder straps were replaced with yellow epaulettes, which were golden for officers. In 1831, the winter trousers became dark blue with a red side-stripe. In 1844, the new Albert shako replaced the previous one, featuring a brass frontal plate and white short plume. In 1855, the old-fashioned tail-coat was replaced with a more practical single-breasted tunic. This was dark blue with red standing collar piped in yellow and dark blue pointed cuffs decorated with a small Hungarian knot in yellow. The front of the tunic was piped in red and had dark blue shoulder straps piped in red. With the introduction of the tunic, the Albert shako was replaced with a busby made of black fur that was similar to that used by the light cavalry. The busby had a red side-bag on the right and white short plume on the left. The outfit was completed by dark blue trousers that had a red side-stripe. The uniform of the foot artillery introduced in 1855 remained practically unchanged until the end of Queen Victoria's reign, except for the substitution of the busby with the new spiked helmet in 1878. The new headgear was dark blue for the artillery and had brass frontal plate as well as brass spike (which was replaced by a brass ball in 1881).

From its formation, the Royal Horse Artillery wore uniforms similar to those of the Light Dragoons. Until 1827, it continued to wear the same dress that it had used during the Napoleonic Wars; this comprised black Tarleton helmet with brass fittings (surmounted by a black crest and having a white plume on the left side), dark blue dolman jacket with red facings (standing collar and pointed cuffs, both piped in yellow) and yellow frontal frogging, and white breeches. In 1827, the Tarleton helmet was replaced by a bell-shaped shako that had yellow decorative cords, white falling plume and brass frontal plate; the white breeches were substituted with dark blue trousers having a red side-stripe. In 1837, the shako was replaced with a busby made of black fur, which had a red side-bag on the right and a white short plume on the front (longer for officers), as well as yellow decorative cords. In 1844, the number of rows of ball buttons on the front of the dolman jacket was increased from three to five. In 1855, the dolman was simplified, with a single row of ball buttons on the front, together with the usual yellow frogging. The jacket's collar was red with

Officers of the Corps of Royal Engineers. The figure on the left is wearing a busby and M1855 tunic, while that on the right is wearing service dress. (*ASKB*)

Artillery and Technical Corps 149

NCOs (left) and private (right) of the Corps of Royal Engineers. The central figure is wearing service dress, while the other two are wearing an M1855 tunic. (*ASKB*)

Private of the Corps of Royal Engineers in 1875. (*ASKB*)

yellow piping and yellow flaming grenade badge, pointed cuffs were dark blue and there were yellow Hungarian knots on the sleeves, as well as yellow boards on the shoulders. The busby remained more or less the same, merely becoming shorter, while thee trousers remained dark blue with a red side-stripe. The uniform introduced in 1855 remained more or less the same until the end of Queen Victoria's reign.

The Royal Engineers and the Royal Sappers and Miners were always dressed like the foot component of the Royal Artillery, albeit in scarlet with dark blue facings. Until 1831, the Royal Sappers and Miners wore a red single-breasted tail-coat having dark blue facings (standing collar and round cuffs), yellow piping to the collar, dark blue shoulder straps piped in yellow and yellow pointed lace loops on the buttonholes of the front and the cuffs. The tail-coat was worn with grey trousers having a red side-stripe. The headgear was a Regency shako with brass frontal plate and white plume, but this was replaced with the M1828 bell-shaped shako. In 1831, a new model of tail-coat was introduced, having two close rows of buttons down the front and cuff flaps with three buttons each. The cuff flaps were red and their buttonholes were laced in yellow; the buttons on the front of the tail-coat did not have yellow lace on their buttonholes. The collar had decorative yellow lace. On the M1831 tail-coat, the previous shoulder straps were replaced with yellow epaulettes, which were golden for officers. From 1831, the winter trousers became dark blue with a red side-stripe. The Royal Staff Corps, until

Artillery and Technical Corps 151

Officer of the Royal Waggon Train wearing an M1828 shako and M1831 tail-coat. (*ASKB*)

its disbandment, was uniformed like the Royal Sappers and Miners. In 1844, the new Albert shako replaced the previous one, having a brass frontal plate and white short plume. In 1855, the old-fashioned tail-coat was replaced with a more practical single-breasted tunic. This was red with dark blue standing collar piped in yellow and dark blue pointed cuffs; the latter were decorated with a small Hungarian knot in yellow. The front of the tunic was piped in dark blue, and had dark blue shoulder straps piped in yellow. With the introduction of the tunic, the Albert shako was replaced with a busby made of black fur that was similar to that used by the foot artillery. The new headgear had a dark blue side-bag on the right and white short plume on the left. The outfit was completed by dark blue trousers that had a red side-stripe. The uniform of the Corps of Royal Engineers introduced in 1855 remained practically unchanged until the death of Queen Victoria, except for the substitution

NCO of the Military Train in 1861. (*ASKB*)

NCO (left) and officer (right) of the Military Train in 1864. (*ASKB*)

of the busby with a spiked helmet in 1878. The new headgear was dark blue, like that of the foot artillery, and had a brass frontal plate and brass spike (the latter being replaced by a brass ball in 1881).

By the time of its disbandment in 1833, the Royal Waggon Train wore the black M1828 shako with white-over-red plume and red double-breasted tail-coat with dark blue facings piped in yellow. The Land Transport Corps formed in 1855 wore a very peculiar uniform: black wide-brimmed hat with turned-up brim on the left side, dark blue double-breasted tunic with light blue standing collar and pointed cuffs, light blue frontal piping and shoulder straps, and dark blue trousers with a light blue side-stripe. The Military Train, from its creation, was uniformed like the line infantry but in dark blue with white facings. Its members wore a shako covered with dark blue cloth and having a black falling plume on the front, as well as a dark blue single-breasted tunic (with white standing collar and shoulder straps) and dark blue trousers that had a white side-stripe. The Army Service Corps inherited the uniform of the Military Train, which remained practically unchanged until the end of Queen Victoria's reign except for the substitution of the shako with the new spiked helmet in 1878. The new headgear was dark blue and had a brass frontal plate as well as a brass spike (the latter replaced by a brass ball in 1881). The Mounted Staff Corps of the Crimean War wore an elegant uniform comprising a black Albert helmet with brass spike, brass frontal plate and black falling plume; scarlet red single-breasted

NCOs of the Military Mounted Police. (*ASKB*)

tunic having dark blue facings and black frontal frogging; and dark blue trousers with red double side-stripe. The Military Mounted Police was uniformed very similarly to the foot component of the Royal Artillery, in dark blue with red facings and having a dark blue spiked helmet. The Military Foot Police adopted the same uniform as the Military Mounted Police.

Chapter 6

Royal Marines

History and Organization

Until 1755, the naval infantry component of the Royal Navy was provided by several infantry regiments that were detached from the rest of the British Army for service at sea. The practice of using normal infantry units to perform naval infantry duties had begun in 1664, when the Duke of York and Albany's Maritime Regiment of Foot was raised. Also known as the Admiral Regiment, it provided infantrymen for several warships of the English Navy. In 1755, the British government decided to organize an independent corps of naval infantry, which received the official denomination of Marines (which was changed to Royal Marines in 1802). The new naval infantrymen were initially structured on fifteen autonomous companies, each of which could be sent to serve on one warship. Differently from the sailors of the Royal Navy, the Marines were all volunteers, like the infantry of the army, with whom they had a lot in common (including their red uniform). The various companies of Marines were split into three divisions that took their name from the location where they were based: Chatham, Portsmouth and Plymouth. In 1805, a fourth division was established at Woolwich. Each division included a different number of companies. At the beginning of Queen Victoria's reign in 1837, there were ninety companies of Royal Marines. Until 1804, the guns of the Royal Navy's warships were manned by the Royal Marines or by the sailors embarked on each vessel, but this could cause serious problems as a specific level of competence was needed to fire naval guns at sea effectively. As a result, in August of that year, a new corps of Royal Marine Artillery was formed, which was part of the Royal Marines but whose members were naval artillerymen rather than naval infantry.

In 1837, the Royal Marine Artillery consisted of just two companies, but by 1854 the Royal Navy had 110 companies of Royal Marines and twelve companies of Royal Marine Artillery. The Royal Marines played a key role during the Crimean War. For instance, once the British expeditionary force reached Crimea, 1,200 of them disembarked and formed a temporary Royal Marines Battalion that fought as regular infantry against the Russians. This was repeated during several campaigns fought by the British in the second half of the nineteenth century. The naval infantry's more

NCO of the Royal Marines wearing an M1828 shako and M1831 tail-coat. (*ASKB*)

Private (left) and officer (right) of the Royal Marines wearing the Albert shako and M1831 tail-coat. (*ASKB*)

Private of the Royal Marines wearing an M1861 shako and M1855 tunic. (*ASKB*)

usual tasks, however, were acting as marksmen on warships, conducting boarding operations and organizing amphibious landings. In addition, they could prevent or crush mutinies among sailors. In January 1855, the Royal Marines received the new name of the Royal Marines Light Infantry, which was amended to the Royal Marine Light Infantry in 1862. Nevertheless, the changes of denomination did not affect the nature of the corps. In 1859, the Royal Navy had 112 companies of Royal Marines and sixteen companies of Royal Marine Artillery, the latter's nickname being the Blue Marines as they were dressed in dark blue like the Royal Artillery rather than the scarlet of the infantry. The 1860s saw a progressive reduction in the number of companies, so that by 1873 there were just forty-eight companies of Red Marines but still sixteen companies of Blue Marines. By the end of Queen Victoria's reign, the Royal Navy could deploy an average of seventy companies of Royal Marines (15,000 men) and twenty-four companies of Royal Marine Artillery (4,000 men).

Uniforms and Equipment

From their creation, the Royal Marines were always dressed similarly to the line infantry in red with dark blue facings. Until 1831, they wore a red single-breasted tail-coat having dark blue facings (standing collar and round cuffs), white piping to the collar, dark blue shoulder straps piped in white and white pointed lace loops on the buttonholes of the front and the cuffs. The tail-coat was worn with grey trousers during cold months and white ones during hot months. The Marines' headgear was a Regency shako with brass frontal plate and white pompom, which was replaced by the M1828 bell-shaped shako. In 1831, a new model of tail-coat was introduced, with two close rows of buttons down the front and cuff flaps. The dark blue collar had decorative white lace, while the dark blue round cuffs had white piping. The new coat had red cuff flaps with three buttons each, the buttonholes having white lace loops. On the M1831 tail-coat, the previous shoulder straps were replaced with brass contre-epaulettes for rankers and golden epaulettes for officers. In 1844, the new Albert shako was introduced, with brass frontal plate and white pompom. In 1855, the old-fashioned tail-coat was replaced with a more practical single-breasted tunic. This was red with dark blue standing collar and round cuffs piped in white; shoulder straps and cuff flaps were dark blue with white piping, the latter having three buttons each and buttonholes with white lace loops. The front of the tunic was piped in white. Trousers became dark blue with a red side-stripe. Following the introduction of the tunic, the Royal Marines were issued with all the new models of shako that were adopted by the line infantry, but with a distinctive green pompom (green became part of the Red Marines' uniforms after they adopted the new official

From left to right: musician, private, officers and NCO of the Royal Marines. All the figures are wearing the M1868 tunic and M1878 spiked helmet. (*ASKB*)

denomination of Royal Marines Light Infantry). In 1868, cuff flaps were abolished and the round cuffs were replaced by new pointed ones (always in dark blue) that were decorated with a small Hungarian knot in white. After these modifications, the uniform of the Royal Marines remained practically unchanged until the end of Queen Victoria's reign, apart from the substitution of the shako by the new spiked helmet in 1878. The new headgear was black and had brass frontal plate as well as brass spike. During the whole period from 1815–1901, the Royal Marine Artillery was always dressed almost identically to the foot component of the Royal Artillery, in dark blue with red facings (hence the corps' nickname of Blue Marines).

Private of the Royal Marines wearing an M1868 tunic and M1878 spiked helmet.

NCO (left) and private (right) of the Royal Marine Artillery wearing the M1868 tunic and M1881 helmet.

Chapter 7

Volunteer Legions and Foreign Units

The South American Wars of Independence, 1817–1825

After the outbreak of the Wars of Independence in South America, the British government provided significant bank loans and massive amounts of weapons to the local insurgents who sought to free themselves from the Spanish colonial yoke. The British had long wanted to see the fall of the Spanish Empire in South America, as with the expulsion of the Spaniards, the commercial monopolies of the colonial period would end and South America would become an immense new market for British merchants (who were extremely interested in purchasing at low cost the region's natural resources). At the end of the Napoleonic Wars in 1815, the British government had to demobilize its massive military forces that had recently helped to defeat Napoleon at Waterloo, so many battle-hardened professional soldiers were going to be discarded by the British Army. The Duke of Wellington, seeking a way to demobilize his army without causing mutinies or revolts, had the idea of sending his unemployed veterans to South America, where they could fight as 'volunteers' in the patriot army of Simón Bolívar. The arrival of thousands of professional British soldiers in Venezuela provided a massive boost for the patriot cause, as these fighters had great combat experience and were perfectly drilled. They soon made up a fundamental component of Bolívar's troops, playing a prominent role in all the most important battles fought by the Gran Colombian Army of the famous Venezuelan general. The officers of the British units acted as instructors for the locally raised patriot corps, making a decisive contribution to the general improvement of their fighting quality. Britain thus provided vital military support to Bolívar's cause without directly entering the conflict. The British veterans who went to South America were engaged on a private basis as volunteers and were paid – at least on paper – by the revolutionary government.

The first British military units went to Venezuela in 1817 and consisted of the following: one battalion of riflemen, two squadrons of hussars, two squadrons of lancers and one company of artillery. The Rifleros Battalion soon became the best unit of Bolívar's infantry, being the only one to be entirely equipped with rifled weapons; it won several battles for the patriot cause and even became part of the elite Bolivarian Guard. The two squadrons of hussars were soon assembled together to form a single unit, which fought with distinction until being absorbed into another corps. The two squadrons of lancers never became active in South America, one of them being lost to a storm during the crossing of the Atlantic Ocean. The artillery company, meanwhile, existed until 1819. After the arrival of the first of these units, further expeditions of British volunteers (named after the officers who had organized them) continued to reach South America throughout 1818 and 1819. The first of these, known as MacGregor's Expedition, comprised two line infantry battalions, one light infantry company, one hussar squadron and one artillery company. The second expedition, known as Elsom's Expedition and comprising a significant number of soldiers who were veterans of the British Army's Hanoverian units, consisted of one rifle battalion and one hussar squadron. The third expedition, English's Expedition, consisted of one line infantry battalion and one hussar regiment. These additional British units arriving in South America, however, were not of the same quality as those that had left Europe in 1817; most of them were quite short-lived and participated in only a few significant engagements. An exception to this rule was the line infantry battalion of English's Expedition, known as the British Legion Battalion, which became part of the Bolivarian Guard. Following the success of the British volunteers in South America, new contingents of veterans and adventurers wishing to fight in the ranks of the Gran Colombian Army started to be raised in Ireland. An entire Irish Legion was formed for service against the Spaniards, which was made up of two battalions of rifles, two battalions of light infantry and one regiment of lancers. However, the Irish Legion lost many of its members due to desertion and tropical diseases soon after crossing the Atlantic; it never reached its planned establishment once in South America and was rapidly disbanded. In October 1819, the surviving elements of the various British corps that had already been disbanded were merged to form a line infantry unit known as the Albion Battalion, which fought with distinction in Ecuador before being dissolved in 1823. In October 1820, the surviving elements of the Irish Legion and various other recently dissolved British units were absorbed into the British Legion Battalion, which then assumed the new denomination of the Cazadores Británicos. This was in turn changed to the Carabobo Battalion in 1821. The unit remained part of the Gran Colombian Army until being disbanded in 1827. By the time of the dissolution of Bolívar's army in 1830, the only remaining British corps of the Gran Colombian Army was the Rifleros Battalion, which had already been completely reorganized with Venezuelan recruits during 1829.

The War of the Two Brothers, 1828–1834

During the first half of the nineteenth century, the British government supported various Liberal political movements in their struggles across the European continent, as the triumph of liberalism in other countries would have only positive effects on the economy and trade of Great Britain. During the 1820s, Britain was strongly involved in the politics of the Iberian countries of Spain and Portugal, which had been freed from French rule by Wellington's British troops just a few years before and thus represented important regional allies for the government in London. Following the end of the Napoleonic Wars, Brazil – Portugal's largest colony – became independent as the Brazilian Empire under the guidance of Pedro I, the eldest son of the King of Portugal, John VI. When his father died in 1826, Pedro I was crowned King of Portugal, but the newly written constitution of Brazil did not permit Pedro to rule over both Portugal and Brazil. As a result, the new monarch was soon forced to abdicate from the Portuguese throne in favour of his infant daughter, Maria, and to return to Brazil. Pedro's younger brother, Miguel, however, did not accept this state of affairs, and – counting on the support of most of the Portuguese military – deposed Maria in a coup in 1828 and had himself crowned King of Portugal. In April 1831, having decided that the time had come to fight against Miguel to enforce the rights of his daughter, Pedro I abdicated as Emperor of Brazil and left South America for Portugal, where he initiated a civil war against his brother. Pedro was supported by the Liberals of his country, while Miguel was the champion of the Portuguese Conservatives.

The former Emperor of Brazil, having to build up an army almost from scratch, relied heavily on the military support that was provided by his British allies. As had already happened during the South American Wars of Independence, several volunteer corps made up of veterans of the Napoleonic Wars were recruited in Britain. These consisted of the following: the Naval Brigade, a unit comprising two regiments of English line infantry; the British Grenadiers, a regiment of British line infantry; the Naval Fusiliers, a regiment of Scottish line infantry comprising a detachment of rifles (the Gentlemen Rifle Cadets); the Grenadiers of the Queen, a regiment of Irish line infantry; and Bacon's Lancers (a small cavalry unit of 200 men, named after its commander). These British military units played a prominent role in the War of the Two Brothers that shattered Portugal between 1828 and 1834, contributing decisively to the final victory of Pedro and the Portuguese liberals.

The First Carlist War, 1833–1840

In 1833, following the death of the Spanish monarch, Ferdinand VII, a bloody civil war broke out in Spain between the country's Liberals and Conservatives. The Liberals recognized as the legitimate heir to the Spanish throne Isabella, the infant daughter of the dead king, while the Conservatives supported the claims to the throne of Charles of Bourbon, the younger brother of Ferdinand VII. The Conservatives were commonly known as Carlists, after their leader, Charles of Bourbon. From the beginning of the conflict, the British government of Lord Palmerston supported the Spanish Liberal cause in every possible way. The Royal Navy blockaded the coastline of northern Spain that was in the hands of the Carlists and transported Liberal troops on several occasions. Meanwhile, the Royal Marines and Royal Marine Artillery launched occasional raids against the Carlists. In June 1835, due to the many victories obtained by the Conservative insurgents, the British government organized a volunteer Auxiliary Legion to join the Liberal forces (being paid by the government in Madrid). George de Lacy Evans was chosen as the commander of this expeditionary force, which was entirely composed of volunteers and mercenaries from the lowest social classes of Britain. The recruiting operations for this new corps proved successful, and the first British contingents landed in Spain in early July 1835. By the end of October, the British Auxiliary Legion had completed its formation and could deploy 7,800 men (3,200 English, 1,800 Scots and 2,800 Irish). These all enlisted into the Spanish Army, but under British conditions of service. The Legion included a total of ten line infantry regiments, each consisting of a single battalion with eight companies. The ten regiments were numbered 1–10: the first four were English, the 5th, 6th and 8th were Scottish and the 7th, 9th and 10th were Irish. The Auxiliary Legion also included a Rifle Regiment of six companies, two regiments of lancers (one English, the other Irish), various artillery elements (a field battery equipped with two guns and two howitzers) and a small Corps of Sappers and Miners that was formed with personnel from the various infantry units. On 5 May 1836, the British Auxiliary Legion was divided into three brigades: English, Scottish and Irish. It was also augmented with the incorporation of a Spanish unit, whose members were known as the Chapelgorris, or Red Caps, and consisted of former Carlist prisoners of war. From time to time – according to the operational needs – various regular contingents of Royal Marines, Royal Marine Artillery, Royal Artillery and Royal Engineers were temporarily attached to the British Auxiliary Legion.

During the Battle of Oriamendi, which was fought on 16 March 1837, the British Legion suffered very high casualties, which led to a general reorganization of the contingent. The surviving elements of each infantry regiment were assembled

Infantry officer of the British Auxiliary Legion that participated in the First Carlist War. The legions made up of British volunteers that were active in South America, Portugal and Spain were all uniformed like those in the contemporary British Army.

Infantryman of the British Auxiliary Legion that participated in the First Carlist War.

together in order to form six new battalions, of which two were English, two were Scottish, one was Irish and one was made up of riflemen. The other branches of service, including cavalry, did not change their organization. The British Auxiliary Legion was enlisted for two years of service, during which it mainly operated from its base of San Sebastián. On 10 June 1837, their enlistment period expired and the corps was disbanded. A number of the men, however, had already expressed their willingness to continue serving in Spain, so on the same day, the British Second Legion was established. This numbered some 1,700 men, who were divided into three infantry battalions (Scottish, Irish and Rifle), one regiment of lancers and some elements of artillery and sappers. The new legion was very short-lived, being disbanded on 8 December 1837. Once again, however, some of the men remained in Spain. These 400 volunteers were reorganized on 1 March 1838 and formed a new British Auxiliary Brigade, consisting of just one regiment of lancers and the artillery inherited from the Second Legion (having four light brass guns and two howitzers). The British military contribution to the Liberal cause was extremely significant and led to the final defeat of the Carlists in 1840. It has been estimated that during the First Carlist War, the British government provided fifty artillery pieces and 350,000 Brown Bess muskets to the Liberals, in addition to an indefinite number of bank loans.

The Foreign Units of the Crimean War

At the beginning of the Crimean War, the British Army experienced a serious shortage of manpower, being much smaller than its Russian opponent as well as its French ally. After the Napoleonic Wars, Britain had greatly reduced its military forces as an economic measure. The British Army had been restructured mostly to perform police and garrison duties across the many colonies that it had to protect. Britain was not ready for a full-scale conflict against a major military power on the European continent. As a result of this, along with British soldiers not being particularly happy about serving for a considerable length of time in an inhospitable and far-off region like Crimea, the British authorities had no choice but to start recruiting units of foreign mercenaries in order to sustain their war effort. Something similar had already happened during the Napoleonic Wars, and the British had the positive example of the French, who had long-since formed their famous and effective Foreign Legion. Britain's new foreign units were recruited from areas of Europe where potential soldiers of fortune were available in great numbers: Switzerland, Germany and Italy. Such regions were all fragmented into small political entities that were completely autonomous but quite weak from a military point of view, making them perfect to provide volunteers for a foreign power like Britain. During the Napoleonic Wars, the British Army had recruited several excellent infantry units from the Swiss cantons, which had a long-established reputation as a homeland for mercenaries. Most of the European armies of the eighteenth and early nineteenth centuries included sizeable contingents of Swiss professional soldiers, and the British military were confident that they could swiftly raise a large Swiss Legion and deploy it in Crimea. The original plan was to form the following Swiss units: eight battalions of light infantry, two battalions of rifles, two regiments of cavalry and some elements of artillery and engineers. During recent years, however, the political situation of Switzerland had changed dramatically following the civil war of 1847 that had seen two alliances of cantons fighting against each other. Since 1852, in fact, the country had adopted a more centralized form of government, the previous cantonal military contingents having been replaced by a unified Swiss Army. The new Helvetic government, soon after its creation, tried to limit as much as possible the practice of foreign states recruiting mercenaries in Switzerland, so the British encountered serious difficulties in finding enough men. The formation of the Swiss Legion began in March 1854, when a recruiting committee and receiving depot were established by the British near Strasbourg, close to the Swiss border. By the end of 1855, however, only two regiments of light infantry, each with two battalions, had been raised from Swiss volunteers. The 1st Regiment and the 1st Battalion of the 2nd Regiment were sent to Smyrna in western Turkey during the early months of 1856, but the Crimean War ended before they could face the Russians. In May 1856, both regiments of the Swiss Legion were disbanded without having seen action and their men were repatriated.

During the Napoleonic Wars, the British Army had raised its best foreign units from Germany, in particular from the state of Hanover, which through the Georgian monarchs had been in a personal union with Britain until the ascendancy of Queen Victoria in 1837. When the Crimean War began, the British authorities soon elaborated plans for the formation of a new German Legion, to be organized similarly to the famous King's German Legion that had fought with distinction in the Napoleonic Wars. The German Prince Albert, consort of Queen Victoria, was enthusiastic about the idea of recruiting a legion from the German princedoms, working hard to assure the success of this project. In November 1854, the British Parliament passed the Foreign Enlistment Act, according to which foreigners could be enlisted in the British Army for the duration of the conflict with Russia and for service outside the British Isles. The recruiting operations for the Germans were easier than those for the Swiss and were organized by the commander of the German Legion, Major General Richard von Stutterheim. He hired 200 recruiting agents in Germany and sent them to the major port cities where large numbers of potential volunteers were available. The recruiters usually went to taverns and bought beer for young adventurers who might be interested in joining the ranks of the legion. By September 1855, von Stutterheim, despite encountering strong opposition from the governments of the German princedoms, had been able to establish six regiments of light infantry with two battalions each, two regiments of rifles with two battalions each and one regiment of cavalry (light dragoons). These were all

From left to right: light infantry officer of the Swiss Legion, rifle officer of the Swiss Legion and light infantry NCO of the Swiss Legion. Two of the figures are wearing the scarlet-red double-breasted M1855 tunic and Albert shako. The three foreign legions formed during the Crimean War were uniformed like the rest of the British Army. The irregulars making up Beatson's Horse wore their traditional civilian clothes, while the officers of the Osmanli Horse Artillery had the red Albert helmet and dark blue jacket with red facings as well as golden frontal frogging and golden Hungarian knots on the sleeves. The officers of the Anglo-Turkish Contingent wore dark blue or red peaked caps having a brass crescent on the front and dark blue shell jackets; the latter had the badge of the Anglo-Turkish Contingent – comprising the monogram of Queen Victoria – embroidered on the right sleeve above the pointed cuff.

sent to training camps in Britain, where they underwent a period of formation. Meanwhile, in Germany, another regiment of rifles was in the process of being formed. Before the Crimean War ended, however, the only units of the German Legion to be dispatched in time to reach the theatre of operations were the 1st, 2nd and 3rd Regiments of Light Infantry and the 1st Regiment of Rifles. None of these saw action, but all suffered losses due to cholera. Upon disbandment of the legion, the German mercenaries could choose to return home (at the expense of the British government) or move to Cape Colony in southern Africa, where they could settle as soldier-colonists. Each German mercenary was to receive an acre of land in exchange for accepting to defend the colony from the attacks of local natives. Around 2,300 German soldiers arrived at the Cape in the early weeks of 1857. They settled down as military colonists and started to be known as the Jager Corps, but never truly adapted to the living conditions of South Africa. In 1858, around 1,400 members of the German Legion – which had not yet formally been disbanded – agreed to leave the Cape and be sent to India in order to fight in the Indian Mutiny. However, once again the Germans arrived too late to play any role in the campaign in India. Around 600 of them returned to South Africa, while the others joined the ranks of the East India Company's European military units. What remained of the German Legion was officially disbanded in 1861, after several of its surviving members had joined the Cape Mounted Riflemen.

According to the original plans for the formation of the three foreign legions, the British authorities were to recruit a total of 20,000 mercenaries: 10,000 Germans, 5,000 Swiss and 5,000 Italians. These numbers looked sufficiently large to avoid the introduction of conscription in Britain, which most of the other European armies already had in order to deploy sizeable military contingents. From the beginning of the Crimean War, Britain could count on the support of the Italian Kingdom of Sardinia (i.e. Piedmont). The Piedmontese were preparing for a war against the Austrian Empire and had ambitions to complete the unification of Italy. The only way for them to win a conflict against the Austrians was to obtain the diplomatic support of Britain and France, hence the decision of the Piedmontese government to enter the Crimean War. The British, in addition to counting on the large expeditionary force sent by the Piedmontese, wanted to recruit an Italian Legion of mercenaries from the other Italian states. With the help of Piedmont, but encountering the strong opposition of the Austrians, the British were able to recruit three regiments of light infantry and one regiment of rifles for the Italian Legion. These were trained in Piedmont, but were ready to fight only when the hostilities with Russia were coming to an end. In 1856, while the Treaty of Paris was about to be signed between the opposing powers, the Italian Legion reached the island of Malta. It was disbanded in the summer of the same year, due to the indiscipline of many of its members (several of whom were former Lombard or Sicilian revolutionaries), without having seen action. As is clear from the above, the foreign legions of mercenaries established for employment in the Crimean War ended up a total failure and made no significant contribution to the British cause. Times had changed since the days of the Napoleonic Wars, the emergence of new nationalistic feelings across Europe having negated the possibility of recruiting effective mercenary contingents.

In addition to recruiting soldiers of fortune from Europe, the British also tried to organize some auxiliary contingents using Ottoman soldiers. First of all, the British made an attempt to discipline the bashi-bazouks, the irregular soldiers of the Ottoman Army, in the hope of transforming them into something comparable to the Indian native cavalry serving under the flags of the East India Company. William Ferguson Beatson, a major serving in the military of the East India Company – later known as Shemshi Pasha – was tasked with forming a semi-disciplined corps of bashi-bazouks that was known as Beatson's Horse, or the Osmanli Irregular Cavalry. Beatson, together with some other capable British officers, recruited a total of 4,000 Ottoman irregulars, who were assembled into a cavalry division, comprising 1,000 Anatolians, 1,000 Syrians, 1,000 Albanians/Bosnians and 1,000 Macedonians. Paid by the British, these men were divided into five regiments that had small cadres of British officers. By the end of 1854, Beatson's Horse was ready to fight, but Lord Raglan (overall commander of the British expeditionary force) was never fully convinced about their combat capabilities and thus never authorized their employment. After some episodes of indiscipline, and due to a chronic lack of funds, Beatson's Horse was finally disbanded in September 1855. During the autumn of 1855, some of the best elements from the disbanded irregular cavalry were re-enlisted by the British to form the new Osmanli Irregular Cavalry, but these never had any proper organization and were disbanded in July 1856 without having seen much action. The British also raised another independent regular corps from Turkish soldiers, the Osmanli Horse Artillery. Consisting of four troops of mounted artillery (equipped with 9-pounder guns and 24-pounder howitzers), they were commanded by twelve British officers (most of whom were former NCOs). Created by Beatson, this corps was intended to be part of Beatson's Horse, but after the latter was disbanded it was attached to the Anglo-Turkish Contingent (see below).

Soon after their arrival in the Ottoman Empire, the British realized that the Turkish infantrymen had great potential as soldiers but that they needed competent officers and NCOs in order to perform well on the battlefield. Consequently, it was agreed with the Ottoman authorities to organize a large Anglo-Turkish Contingent, an infantry force consisting of Turkish soldiers trained and commanded by British officers and NCOs. The basic idea was to create a Westernized Ottoman contingent that would be very similar to the military forces of the East India Company: some entire regiments of Turkish line infantry were to be transferred to British service after having been deprived of their own incompetent leadership. The Ottoman authorities were not particularly enthusiast about the idea of ceding some of their best soldiers to the British, but in the end they had no choice but to accept the proposal. By August 1855, the Anglo-Turkish Contingent consisted of ten regiments of line infantry, two regiments of cavalry and four batteries of artillery. Of these, seven regiments of line infantry, both units of cavalry and one battery of artillery came from the *Redeef* (Reserve) of the Ottoman Army rather than the Turkish regular forces. After a few months, the Anglo-Turkish Contingent received its definitive organization; it consisted of sixteen regiments of line infantry assembled into four brigades with four regiments each, three regiments of cavalry, six batteries of foot artillery, one battery of horse artillery, one battery of garrison artillery, one engineer corps (including a small telegraph detachment) and one transport corps. Most of the officers who commanded these various units came from the armies of the East India Company and had enlisted into the Anglo-Turkish Contingent to obtain 'easy' promotions while serving within the Ottoman Army, with lieutenant colonels becoming colonels, majors becoming lieutenant colonels, captains becoming majors and lieutenants becoming captains. The new brevets received by these officers resulted in higher pay, which was provided by the British authorities. The 17,000 men of the Anglo-Turkish Contingent mostly performed auxiliary duties during the closing months of the Crimean War, including garrisoning important locations, and the corps was finally disbanded in May 1856.

Chapter 8

The Crimean War, 1853–1856

By the beginning of the nineteenth century, the Ottoman Empire was the 'sick man of Europe' following a long phase of decline that had begun at the end of the seventeenth century. The Ottoman Turks, having been a major military power of the European continent for centuries, had entered an age of crushing military defeats that resulted in the secession of several areas of the Ottoman Empire. For two centuries, the Turks controlled most of the Balkans as well as the Middle East, ruling over a multi-ethnic empire that extended from Bosnia and Romania in the Balkans to Iraq and Arabia in the Middle East. Ottoman lands also included vast portions of Muslim North Africa, from Algeria in the west to Egypt in the east. During the period of the Napoleonic Wars, however, the Turks failed to modernize their military forces along western lines, which led to a series of defeats. Situated around the Ottoman Empire were several foreign powers that sought to take advantage of the Turks' decline in order to enlarge their domains: Austria and Russia had long desired to expel the Ottomans from the Balkans, while Great Britain and France wanted to exert their control over the Mediterranean by reducing the power of the Turks. Furthermore, the Ottoman Empire was shattered by various secessionist movements: in the Balkan territories, in particular, there were several national communities ready to fight in order to obtain their independence. Some of these already enjoyed a high degree of autonomy within the Ottoman Empire, including the Principality of Serbia and the Danubian Principalities of Moldavia and Wallachia that made up present-day Romania. During the early decades of the nineteenth century, these vassal states of the Ottomans became practically independent, while Greece rose up in revolt against the Turks by initiating a long and bloody war of independence (1821–30). The Greeks were openly supported in their struggle by Britain, France and Russia, whose combined naval forces destroyed the Ottoman Navy at the Battle of Navarino in 1827 and thus secured victory for the Greek cause. The French sent an expeditionary corps to Greece and in 1830 invaded Ottoman Algeria, transforming the North African territory into one of their colonies. The Russians, meanwhile, temporarily invaded the Danubian Principalities and also attacked the Turks in the Caucasus.

Following these events, the Ottoman Empire risked collapse since it was unable to preserve its territorial integrity. Egypt, which had long been one of the key Turkish domains, seceded from the Ottoman Empire and rapidly became a significant regional power of the Middle East. The Russians, at the same time, nurtured ambitions to conquer most of the southern Balkans for themselves. However, Britain, which was the dominant naval power in the Mediterranean, was keen to avoid the complete collapse of the Turkish state, the British government being well aware that this would have increased the influence of Russia, which would have been able to obtain an outlet to the Mediterranean for its expanding fleet. The Ottomans, from their capital of Constantinople, controlled the strategic Dardanelles Strait that connected the Black Sea with the Mediterranean. For British commercial and military interests, it was absolutely vital to avoid the Russians taking control of the naval routes passing through the Dardanelles. The rivalry between Britain and Russia for control of the eastern Mediterranean worsened over time, becoming part of what was known as the Eastern Question (a larger process that saw the unstoppable decline of the Turkish state). The British wanted to keep the Ottoman Empire alive in order to prevent the further ascendancy of Russia, whereas the Russians wanted to destroy the Ottoman state once and for all. By the beginning of the 1850s, the Eastern Question came to a turning point, the military and financial weakness of the Ottoman Empire having become apparent. Russia, hoping to take advantage of this, schemed to attack the Turks with the objective of conquering lands in both the Balkans and the Caucasus to the east of the Black Sea. The Russians presented themselves as the defenders of Christian communities that lived inside the Ottoman Empire, as they had already done with Serbia and Greece; their plan was to use religious pretexts as a *casus belli* to invade the Balkans (notably the Danubian Principalities).

The Crimean War commenced in the summer of 1853, when the Russian Army invaded Moldavia and Wallachia without encountering any significant resistance. During the following months, the Russians tried to convince the other great powers to acknowledge the legitimacy of their Balkan conquests, but without success. After the Russian Navy crushed the Ottoman fleet at the Battle of Sinope (30 November 1853), both Britain and France decided to intervene in the conflict in order to prevent the total collapse of the Turks. After some failed negotiations, both powers declared war on Russia on 28 March 1854. The allies immediately sent their naval forces to the Dardanelles and started building new defences there, in order to prevent the Russian Navy in the Black Sea from entering into the Mediterranean. In June 1854, an expeditionary force made up of British and French troops disembarked at Varna, on the coastline of the eastern Balkans, to support the Ottoman Army that was fighting against the Russians along the Danube. Before the allies could organize a counter-offensive, however, the Russian troops left the Danubian Principalities after Austria threatened to join the allies in the conflict. The Austrians mobilized a large army which they deployed in Transylvania, with the intention of attacking the Russians from the west. Russia, being in no condition to face three major enemies at the same time, was keen to avoid an enlargement of the war, partly due to epidemics that had recently killed thousands of its soldiers in the Balkans. After the Russians evacuated the Danubian Principalities, these lands were occupied by Austrian troops, who remained in Romania as a peace keeping force for the rest of the hostilities. Following these events, the allies found themselves in a quite difficult situation: now that the Russians had abandoned the Balkans, they had to find a new way to attack Russia. After high-level discussions, it was finally decided to conduct an offensive operation against the Crimean Peninsula in southern Ukraine, which housed the strategically important port of Sevastopol, the main base of the Russian naval forces deployed in the Black Sea. The allies landed an expeditionary force in Crimea without encountering any strong opposition, but they soon came to understand that Sevastopol was a formidable stronghold.

Before besieging Sevastopol, the allies had to face the Russian forces deployed in Crimea at the Battle of the Alma (20 September 1854). This clash was fought on the Alma Heights, the main natural barrier defending Sevastopol from a land attack. The battle ended up as a hard-won victory for the allies, who could then start encircling Sevastopol, which was soon bombarded from the sea by British and French warships. On 25 October, the Russian Army launched a major assault against the allied positions in the hope of relieving Sevastopol. This resulted in the Battle of Balaclava, which became one of the most famous clashes ever fought by the British Army. During the first phase of the battle, the 93rd Highlanders – despite being seriously outnumbered – repulsed a massive Russian cavalry charge. This episode gave birth to the legend of the 'Thin Red Line', recalling the Highlanders' determination and courage in standing firm against the odds. After the Russian assault was repelled, the Heavy Brigade of the British cavalry counter-attacked and fought hand-to-hand with the enemy's mounted troops, eventually forcing them to retreat. The Russians abandoned several artillery batteries during their withdrawal, which were located on heights that dominated the battlefield. Lord Raglan, the overall commander of the British forces, then ordered the Light Brigade of the British cavalry to capture the abandoned guns. The Light Brigade, however, could not see these batteries, as it was deployed in a nearby valley; the only guns that it could see were on its left and were still manned by Russians who had not been attacked in that sector of the battlefield. As a result, due to a series of mistakes relating to the communication of Raglan's orders, the Light Brigade charged against the wrong enemy batteries. The British light cavalry were decimated by the fire of the Russian guns while riding across what later became known as the Valley of Death. They were able to reach the enemy batteries and kill most of the Russian gunners, but were forced to fall back by counter-attacking Russian Cossacks. The Charge of the Light Brigade had been a disaster for the British Army, but despite this the Battle of Balaklava could not be considered as a defeat for the allies.

On 4 November 1854, the Russian Army launched another major counter-offensive against the allies' positions by crossing the Chernaya River. The Russians had a clear numerical superiority, but during the subsequent Battle of Inkerman all their efforts to break the enemy lines ended in failure. The British and the French fought with enormous courage and – mostly thanks to their superior firepower – were able to cause serious losses to the Russians. Having been defeated at Inkerman, the Russians made no further large-scale attempts to defeat the allies in the field, leaving the British and French to concentrate all their forces against Sevastopol. The siege of the Russian stronghold proved extremely difficult for the allies, who – during the winter of 1854–55 – suffered many hardships and were decimated by epidemics. In June 1855, the British and French launched their first full-scale assault against the enemy positions, but were repulsed, the Russians defending their positions with great determination. The key position for the defenders was the heavily fortified Malakoff Hill. Meanwhile, the Kingdom of Sardinia (i.e. Piedmont) joined the allies and sent a sizeable military force to Crimea. The newly arrived Piedmontese troops helped the British and French in repulsing a Russian counter-offensive at the Battle of the Chernaya. On 5 September 1855, the French were finally able to take Malakoff Hill after a desperate assault; four days later Sevastopol fell, bringing to an end a siege that had lasted 337 days. With both sides now exhausted, and the coming of winter, no further operations took place in Crimea after the surrender of Sevastopol. The allies, however, conducted a series of naval bombardments and minor incursions against Russian positions located in the Sea of Azov (especially around the Kerch Strait, linking Crimea to the southern Russian mainland).

The Crimean War, despite its name, was not fought only in the Crimean Peninsula, action also taking place in several other secondary theatres. In the Caucasus, the Ottomans and Russians had confronted each other since the autumn of 1853 without achieving any significant result. The Russian troops, despite being superior to the Turks in terms of firepower and training, never had the resources to conduct a large-scale offensive in the Caucasus, a region inhabited by various populations that had long been struggling against the Russians for their independence. The Caucasian communities sided with the Ottomans, obliging the Russians to adopt a defensive attitude. Another secondary theatre of the Crimean War was the Baltic Sea, which was entered by an Anglo-French fleet in April 1854. The allied naval forces blockaded Russian trade in the Baltic region and bombarded several enemy coastal fortifications, especially in the Gulf of Finland. Russia depended on imports both for its domestic economy and for the supply of its military forces, meaning that the blockade of the Baltic Sea enacted by the allies seriously undermined Russian financial capabilities. In August 1854, an Anglo-French naval force captured and destroyed the Russian fortress of Bomarsund on the Aland Islands, while a year later, the allies bombarded the fortified Russian dockyards at Sveaborg (just outside Helsinki in Finland). By the time of Sevastopol's fall, the British and French navies were planning a massive assault against Kronstadt, the main base of Russia's Baltic Fleet. The Crimean War was also fought in the Pacific Ocean, where the Russian settlement of Petropavlovsk – located in the Kamchatka Peninsula of Siberia – was besieged by the allies. Several small landings were made by the allies on Sakhalin Island and the Kuril Islands, mostly to prevent any Russian action directed against British Canada. The peace negotiations that brought the Crimean War to an end began in February 1856 and led to the signing of the Treaty of Paris on 30 March of the same year. According to the treaty, the Danubian Principalities became de facto independent from both Turkey and Russia, while the Russians were forced to demilitarize the northern coastline of the Black Sea in exchange for the allies' evacuation of the Crimean Peninsula. The Crimean War was the only major European war fought by the British Army during the reign of Queen Victoria and the last conflict fought on the continent by British troops until the outbreak of the First World War in 1914.

Chapter 9

The Indian Campaigns of the British Army

The Third Anglo-Maratha War, 1817–1818

The British presence in India only started to be significant from the middle of the eighteenth century, particularly after the Battle of Plassey that was fought in 1757. Prior to this, other European colonial powers such as France and Portugal had exerted greater influence over India than Britain. Since the times of its first territorial acquisitions in the Indian subcontinent, the British government had not annexed any Indian territory as a direct possession of the Crown; from a formal and practical point of view, the British territories in India were all under control of the East India Company. Established in 1600, the East India Company was a joint-stock company whose original main objective was trading with the rich countries of the Asian continent. Like its Dutch equivalent operating in present-day Indonesia, the British East India Company gradually emerged as a regional power in Asia and expanded its commercial influence by using political and military measures. The British traders eventually started to occupy some of the important cities of India as well as various tracts of coastline. All these new territories were to act as outposts for the economic activities of the East India Company and were also the centres from which the British could exert their political influence over the local Indian rulers. By the middle of the eighteenth century, with the decline of the great Moghul Empire, India was fractured into a multitude of independent princedoms. These had outdated armies using traditional Indian weaponry and tactics, which were greatly inferior to the modern military technologies employed by the British. As a result of this situation, the East India Company gradually used its great economic resources to transform several of the Indian native states into protectorates. Thanks to the signing of favourable trade treaties, the British acquired direct control over an increasing number of cities and territories. After the victory of Plassey, with which the French were expelled from most of India, the British could expand their possessions towards the interior of the subcontinent. Following the fall of the Moghul Empire, the new major local power of India was the Maratha Empire. Controlling a large portion of central India, the Maratha Empire consisted of a confederation of five different political entities that often had contrasting interests. Between 1775 and 1782, the

British fought the Maratha Empire in what became known as the First Anglo-Maratha War. This proved to be indecisive, neither side obtaining any clear-cut victories. After a major civil war broke out in the Maratha Empire during 1802, the British launched a massive invasion of Maratha territories with 53,000 men. Major General Arthur Wellesley (the future Duke of Wellington) was the main British commander during this Second Anglo-Maratha War, tasked with conquering the vast plains of Deccan. On 23 September 1803, at the Battle of Assaye, Wellesley defeated more than 50,000 Maratha troops with just 10,000 men. By December 1803, most of the Maratha strongholds had been conquered by the British, but the hostilities continued for another two years until the last pockets of resistance were crushed. At the end of the conflict, large portions of the Maratha Empire were annexed by the East India Company. Nevertheless, the company had to fight a Third Anglo-Maratha War from 1817–19, which saw the British secure several victories and ended with the final dissolution of the Maratha Empire.

The Anglo-Burmese Wars, 1824–1886

In 1824, the military capabilities of the East India Company were put to the test after Burmese expansion into the Indian regions of Manipur and Assam created a long border between British-ruled India and the aggressive Burmese Empire. For most of the eighteenth century, the Burmese Empire had been a leading military power in Indochina and had fought several bloody wars against the Thai state of Siam. The Burmese had ambitions to expand into north-eastern India and did not fear any military reaction by the East India Company, being able to deploy a sizeable army that was well trained and partly equipped with modern firearms purchased from Britain's colonial rivals. In 1822, the British authorities in Calcutta began supporting insurgents from Manipur and Assam who resented Burmese rule, providing them with weapons and supplies. The Burmese responded by launching small-scale incursions against the frontier of the British territories. Tensions rapidly grew, to the point that the Burmese deployed most of their armed forces in Manipur and Assam in anticipation of a direct confrontation with Britain. In September 1823, with war seeming inevitable, the Burmese occupied Shalpuri Island near Chittagong. The island had been claimed by the East India Company, and its conquest by Burmese soldiers led to the outbreak of the First Anglo-Burmese War. Hostilities officially began on 5 March 1824, following some border skirmishes between East India Company soldiers and Burmese forces in Arakan. Britain was particularly worried by Burmese expansionism because of the positive relations that existed between the Burmese court and France, which was seeking to exert an increasing influence over the Burmese Empire. The Burmese Army, at least on paper, was one of the largest and most effective native military forces in Asia. For the war with Great Britain it mobilized 10,000 veteran infantry and 500 cavalry, who were commanded by experienced leaders. Burmese war plans were based on attacking the British in Arakan from the south-east and in Cachar from the north-east. In the early phase of the hostilities, the Burmese were able to push back the British forces facing them because they were familiar with fighting in the jungle environment of north-eastern India. British troops moved very slowly across the contested area's dense woodland and had limited knowledge of the local terrain. On 17 May 1824, they were defeated by the Burmese at the Battle of Ramu, the victors fighting their way into the Bengal Presidency. At this point of the conflict, the two Burmese invading columns joined forces and seemed ready to invade British Bengal. The East India Company responded by sending all its warships to the Bengal coast and requesting help from the British government.

With the city of Calcutta having been threatened by Burmese troops, the British had assembled an elite expeditionary force of 10,000 men (5,000 British soldiers and 5,000 sepoys) for an attack against the Burmese mainland. The force consisted of seven regiments of foot from the British Army, one European infantry battalion and twelve native infantry regiments from the Madras Army, three native infantry regiments from the Bengal Army and detachments of artillery and sappers. On 11 May 1824, the British force entered the harbour of Rangoon, the Burmese capital, taking the local forces by surprise. They soon took up position in the large Shwedagon Pagoda and fortified it, and from this new base they expelled the Burmese from Rangoon and obtained a series of minor victories. With a British army on their national soil, the Burmese had no choice but to suspend their invasion of Bengal. By November 1824, the Burmese had assembled 30,000 troops outside their capital as they strove to reconquer it. They launched several violent frontal assaults on the British positions, which were all repulsed with severe losses. In March 1825, the British attacked what remained of the Burmese forces at Danubyu, where the Burmese had built a fortified camp defended by 10,000 soldiers. After some weeks of intense fighting, the Burmese troops were crushed on 1 April and their defensive positions were destroyed. Meanwhile, in Bengal, the British launched a counter-offensive against the last Burmese troops remaining in the region, overcoming them and occupying the Arakan region. On 17 September, a month-long armistice was concluded after the British had also expelled the Burmese from the border region of Assam. Hostilities resumed at the end of the armistice after the failure of peace talks. In November, the Burmese assembled all their remaining forces to fight a last battle against the British, hoping to obtain a victory before the end of the war. The British, however, attacked them first on 1 December at Prome, which resulted in a great victory for the British and the Burmese being forced to surrender. In February 1826, the signing of the Treaty of Yandabo marked the end of the First Anglo-Burmese War. According to its terms, the Burmese Empire ceded to the British several border regions of its territory (Assam, Manipur, Arakan and Tenasserim) and paid a large war indemnity. The outcome of the First Anglo-Burmese War practically destroyed the finances of the Burmese Empire, but the conflict also came at a high human cost for the British, who lost around 15,000 men, mostly to tropical diseases. The loss of their rich frontier territories was particularly humiliating for the Burmese, who fought another two wars against the British in 1852 and 1885. The Second Anglo-Burmese War saw a new British attack against Rangoon and ended with the British annexation of more territories in Lower Burma. The Third Anglo-Burmese War lasted for just a few weeks, resulting in the transformation of Burma into a British colony (although some Burmese armed resistance continued until 1895).

The Anglo-Afghan Wars and Anglo-Persian War, 1839–1880

During the early decades of the eighteenth century, a series of capable politico-military leaders emerged on the territory of present-day Afghanistan, all fighting to create a new nation independent from both Persia and India. Until then, most Afghan lands had been dominated by the various dynasties that had ruled over Persia. In 1747, after several years fighting against their much more powerful enemies, the Afghans were finally able to establish their first independent national state under the guidance of Ahmad Shāh Durrānī. The latter not only unified the Afghan lands under his rule, but transformed his young country into a significant regional power in Central Asia. Prior to this, the various ethnic groups living on the territory of Afghanistan had never pursued common interests and had spent most of their energies in bloody inter-tribal conflicts that favoured foreign powers like Persia or India. Under Ahmad Shāh Durrānī, this situation changed, all the various ethnic components of Afghanistan starting to collaborate in order to defend and expand their homeland. Ahmad Shāh Durrānī submitted most of the nomadic tribes living in northern Afghanistan – Tajiks, Uzbeks and Turkmen – but also made conquests southwards by defeating the Mughal Empire of India on several occasions. In 1757, he even sacked the rich city of Delhi, extending his political authority over Punjab and Kashmir. From 1762, however, the newly established Durrānī Empire started to experience serious difficulties and gradually lost control over some peripheral areas: in the north, the Uzbeks partly restored their autonomy, while Afghan troops were expelled from Punjab by the warlike Sikhs. The Durrānī Dynasty continued to rule over Afghanistan until 1823, but by then most of Ahmad Shāh Durrānī's conquests had been lost by his inept successors. Afghanistan entered a new historical phase of politico-military decay, characterized by the outbreak of frequent civil wars. During the 1830s, the Russian Empire started expanding towards Central Asia, which was perceived by the East India Company as a serious potential threat to its interests in the region. In 1837, in order to form an alliance against the Russians, the company sent an envoy to Kabul, the capital of Afghanistan, seeking a treaty with the local ruler, Dost Mohammad Khan. Afghanistan had recently lost the important city of Peshawar to the Sikh Empire, and thus was willing to form an alliance with Britain. However, the British authorities in India then decided to change their diplomatic attitude towards Afghanistan and to form an alliance with the Sikhs. Having lost the political support of the East India Company, Khan turned to Russia and invited a Russian representative to Kabul. On 20 January 1838, Lord Auckland, Governor-General of British India, sent an ultimatum to Khan asking him to desist from any further diplomatic contact with Russia. The Afghan leader, offended by the ultimatum, expelled the British diplomats from Afghanistan on 26 April. In the following months, Afghanistan was attacked by another enemy, Persia, which was ruled by the Russian-backed Qajar dynasty. A Persian army invaded some border regions of Afghanistan and besieged the important city of Herat, which had been part of Persia until 1709. After considering the new military situation, Lord Auckland decided to intervene in Afghanistan to achieve two distinct political objectives: repulsing the expansionism of the Russian-backed Persians and replacing Khan with a new ruler favourable to British influence over Afghanistan.

Several months later, the Persians abandoned the siege of Herat and returned to their own territory, but the military machine of the East India Company was by then already working at full speed. On 25 November 1838, the two most powerful armies of the Indian subcontinent, those of the Sikh Empire and the East India Company, assembled their forces and started their long march towards Afghanistan. By late March 1839, the British troops had crossed the Bolan Pass and had begun their advance against Kabul, marching through rough terrain, across desert areas and at an altitude of 4,000 metres. Before investing the Afghan capital, the British had to attack the fortress of Ghazni, the key position of the Afghan defensive system, which was captured on 22 July thanks to a surprise attack. In August, the British forces reached Kabul and placed their own pretender on the Afghan throne; apparently the war was over, but Khan had survived and was organizing a guerrilla war against the British invaders. The first year of guerrilla operations was a difficult one for the Afghan resistance forces, which were defeated on several occasions. It became clear, however, that the 8,000 British soldiers who remained in Afghanistan were not enough to face any popular revolt. Between April and October 1841, most of the disaffected Afghan tribes started to actively support Akbar Khan, son of Dost Mohammad Khan and new leader of the resistance. On 2 November, the population of Kabul rose in open revolt against the British garrison. The initial response of the occupation forces, led by General Elphinstone, was extremely slow, allowing the Afghan insurgents to expand their control over large areas of the city. Two months later, the British situation in Kabul having seriously deteriorated, an agreement was finally reached with Akbar Khan, according to which the British troops could abandon Afghanistan and would not be attacked during their retreat towards India. The British column leaving Kabul comprised just 4,500 soldiers, but also included some 12,000 camp followers (mostly women), who greatly slowed down the movements of the retreating army. Soon after abandoning Kabul, the British column was attacked by warriors of the local tribes while struggling through the snowbound mountain passes. All supplies of food and baggage were lost during the early phase of the retreat, while the very cold temperatures, especially at night, caused many losses. While attempting to cross the Koord-Kabual pass in the Hindu Kush, Elphinstone's army was attacked by the local Afghan tribes. The following days were terrible for the British column: during the crossing of another pass, that of Tunghee Tareekee, it was attacked again by the Afghan tribesmen and suffered severe losses. On the evening of 11 January, Elphinstone was captured during peace talks with Akbar Khan. The surviving elements of the British column were finally massacred in the Gandmark Pass, despite showing incredible courage during their last desperate resistance. Of the 16,500 soldiers and camp followers who had left Kabul in early January, not one reached safety in British India. During the spring of 1842, a British military force was sent to Afghanistan and defeated Akbar Khan near the city of Jalalabad, but the new Governor-General of India had orders to end the war as soon as possible after carrying out a few symbolic reprisals. During late summer, Ghazni was again conquered by the British and its fortifications were destroyed, while Kabul was occupied once more in September. A month later, having rescued the British prisoners and having demolished Kabul's main bazaar as an act of retaliation, the British abandoned Afghanistan and the First Anglo-Afghan War came to an end.

During the second half of the nineteenth century, especially after the end of the Crimean War, Russia turned its attention to Central Asia, where it initiated a process of expansion. For several centuries, the Russians already had a presence in the northern part of Central Asia, but were interested in moving southwards in order to exert their political influence over key nations like Persia and Afghanistan. Great Britain, having defeated the Sikhs in the 1840s and assumed control over present-day Pakistan, perceived the Russian expansionist plans as a direct threat to its colonial rule in India. As a result, from the 1850s, the Great Game began in Central Asia between the British and Russian empires. This confrontation, a type of cold war that did not involve a direct clash between the two opponents, mostly took place in Persia and Afghanistan, which soon became bones of contention between the two great powers. Both the Russians and the British wanted to transform the Persian Empire into a buffer zone between their territorial possessions in Asia, but the Qajar Dynasty that ruled over the Persian state had no intention of renouncing its traditional political ambitions. For centuries, the Qajars had been an important regional power in both the Middle East and Central Asia. Persia had, in particular, exerted direct influence over Afghanistan until the beginning of the eighteenth century. The Qajars had their powerbase in present-day Azerbaijan, in the southern part of the Caucasus, where they clashed with the expanding Russians, who had already annexed Georgia during the eighteenth century. In order to face the Russians on almost equal terms, the Persians initiated a process of modernization of their army during the Napoleonic Wars. They did so by inviting a French military mission to their country, which was authorized by Napoleon, who wished to form an anti-British alliance with the Qajars. The French instructors reorganized the Persian armed forces as two separate branches of service: the Sarbaz and the Janbaz. The Sarbaz was based in Azerbaijan and mostly consisted of Caucasian soldiers, its main function being fighting against the Russians. The Janbaz had its most important units garrisoned in Tehran – including the Imperial Guard of the Shah – and was fully mobilized only in case of military emergency. The Westernized infantry of the Sarbaz was organized by the French on *fuadji*, or regiments, which consisted of a single battalion with ten companies. In peacetime, the members of these regiments spent half of the year at home on leave and the other six months training. In 1809, a British military mission entered Qajar service, replacing the French one. The British instructors, mostly experienced officers and NCOs from the military of the East India Company, continued the process of modernization initiated by the French, significantly improving the general quality of the Sarbaz infantry. By 1815, the British instructors had organized the infantry of the Sarbaz on eighteen battalion-sized regiments with ten companies each, while the elite infantry of the Imperial Guard consisted of four battalion-sized regiments. The British military mission also tried to Westernize a number of Qajar cavalrymen, but with little success; by 1815, only four squadrons of European-style cavalry had been established. Regarding artillery, the British instructors from the East India Company achieved significant results. They formed a regular corps of mounted artillery with 1,200 men, who were arranged in ten batteries, each with six guns and 120 soldiers. The traditional artillery of the Janbaz included a distinct branch of camel-mounted artillery equipped with small-calibre bronze guns known as zambureks, from the Persian word *zambur*, meaning wasp. The camel-mounted light artillery was mostly tasked with skirmishing from a distance in order to harass their enemies. The zambureks were falconet cannons fitted with a heavy wooden stock in order to be fired from the back of a kneeling camel, and were transported in wooden saddles with high arches and a felt pillow in the middle.

In the complex political context of the Great Game, Britain was determined to oppose any Qajar attempt to expand Persia's borders. Persia comprised twelve provinces that were mostly inhabited by non-Persians and exerted control over the important naval routes that crossed the Persian Gulf. In 1801, Britain and Qajar Persia signed an important treaty, according to which the British would support the Persians in case of a Russian invasion of the southern Caucasus. In exchange for this, the Qajars agreed to respect the full autonomy of Afghanistan. Over time, however, it became clear that neither of the signatories were interested in respecting the treaty: the British did not help Persia when it was attacked by Russia between 1826 and 1828, while the Qajars continued to play a covert role in the internal politics of Afghanistan. Anglo-Persian relations worsened during the mid-nineteenth century, especially after British troops were defeated in the Anglo-Afghan War of 1839–42. The Qajars wanted to free themselves of all foreign influence and to show their rivals that the Persian Army was still capable of conquering more lands. As a result, on 25 October 1856, Qajar troops occupied the important Afghan city of Herat after having advanced rapidly across western Afghanistan. This was a clear violation of the Anglo-Persian treaty of 1801, to which the British Governor-General of India responded – acting on orders from London – by declaring war on Qajar Persia on 1 November 1856. When the Anglo-Persian conflict began, the Persian Army represented a formidable enemy for the British due to its size. Following the end of hostilities with Russia in 1828, the Sarbaz was disbanded and what remained of it was absorbed into the traditional Persian military. During 1851 and 1852, the Persian Army was reorganized by an Austrian military mission, which introduced a new recruiting system. The whole of Persia was divided into military districts, each of which was required to provide a number of recruits to the central government. Thanks to the introduction of this new system, the Persian regular infantry could be restructured on ten *touman*, or divisions, each consisting of ten battalion-sized regiments. In addition to the 100 line infantry regiments – dressed in Western-style uniforms – there were two elite foot regiments in the Imperial Guard and two regiments made up of Russian deserters, the latter being disbanded after the Crimean War. The regular cavalry continued to be extremely small, consisting of just 500 troopers assembled into a single squadron. The artillery was structured on six battalion-sized regiments of 1,000 men each. The Qajar regular forces, in case of war, were to be supported by large numbers of irregular infantrymen still equipped with old-fashioned matchlock muskets. The regular infantry was armed with flintlock weapons purchased during the Napoleonic Wars; these were British Brown Bess muskets or French Charlevilles. Almost the entire Persian cavalry still consisted of traditional contingents having a semi-regular nature at best.

After declaring war on Persia, the British military authorities in India had to decide how to attack the Qajars in the most effective way. Marching through Afghanistan to expel the Persians from Herat was logistically impossible, because the British could not count on the support of the Afghan tribal rulers. The government in London also wanted to defeat the Qajars, but without causing the fall of their dynasty. Indeed, it was in Britain's interest to have a stable government in Persia that could deter prospective advances by Russia. Following discussions, it was decided to attack Qajar Persia via the Persian Gulf, conducting a punitive expedition rather than a full-scale invasion. After the experiences of the First Anglo-Afghan War, the British government was reluctant to carry out major offensive operations in Central Asia or to commit large numbers of troops for a punitive expedition that was considered as of secondary importance. Initially, the army of the Bombay Presidency was ordered to mobilize a single division for the campaign against the Qajar Empire, consisting of 2,300 British and 3,400 Indian soldiers, who landed on the southern coastline of Persia in early December 1856. It soon became apparent that a second division was needed to carry on an effective military operation. This second force, commanded by Brigadier General Henry Havelock, joined the original division in January 1857. The British expeditionary force captured the island of Kharag on 4 December before landing on the Persian mainland just a few miles south of the important port of Bushire, which was captured after a short but effective naval bombardment. The British troops then temporarily halted their offensive to await the arrival of Havelock's division. After the reinforcements turned up, overall command of the British expeditionary force was assigned to Sir James Outram of the Bombay Army. The British troops mostly consisted of the following units provided by the East India Company, being part of the Bombay Army: the 64th Regiment of Foot, 78th Highlanders, 2nd Bombay European Infantry, 4th, 20th, 23rd and 26th Bombay Native Infantry, 14th Regiment of Light Dragoons, 3rd Bombay Native Cavalry, Scinde Horse and Poona Horse (irregular Indian cavalry formations), two batteries of foot artillery, one battery of horse artillery and detachments of sappers and miners from the Bombay Army and Madras Army. On 3 February 1857, the British troops, divided into two columns that maintained the same distance between themselves, marched towards the interior but were soon discovered by a small party of Qajar cavalry. The Persians had prepared a defensive position, mounting eighteen guns at Borazjan, and during recent weeks had mobilized most of their regular infantry for a large-scale confrontation with the invaders. The Qajar commanders did not have a precise idea of the size of the British forces, so after spotting them on the march they decided to withdraw from Borazjan in order to gain time and gather more infantry regiments. The British numbered around 14,000 men and had twenty-eight guns, and the Qajars would have been able to face them only if having a substantial numerical superiority. The hasty Persian retreat left large amounts of ammunition and supplies in the hands of the advancing British. After taking Borazjan, the British retired to their main base of Bushire but were harassed by a contingent of Qajar irregular cavalry. The British rearguard was involved in a series of minor skirmishes, which were of no practical importance but did slow down the movements of the British. While these events took place, a new Persian force of 8,000 men was assembled and sent to the theatre of operations.

On 8 February, with the Qajar forces now numerous enough to face the British, they decided to fight in the open field against the invaders, who were encamped at Khoshab. The battle began with the fire of the opposing artilleries, which was not very accurate on the Persian side. The British deployed their infantry in two lines and advanced against the enemy centre, where most of the Qajar artillery was concentrated. The British mounted troops, meanwhile, attacked the Persian cavalry on the left, with the decisive support of their horse artillery. This British cavalry attack was successful, meaning the Persian regular infantry then came under attack from two sides. However, the Qajar soldiers proved disciplined and determined, forming a defensive square to halt the attack of the British cavalry. Nevertheless, the Poona Horse managed to break through the Persian ranks and capture the flag of one of the Qajar regiments. This flag was surmounted by a silver hand – a Muslim religious symbol – which was later adopted as a regimental distinction by the Poona Horse. With it becoming apparent that the battle was lost, the Persian infantry began fleeing in disorder and abandoned most of their artillery. The Battle of Khoshab was a major victory for the British, but Outram decided to fall back on Bushire, as he had planned to do before the clash. Although the British movement was hampered by torrential rains, which created deep mud, most of Outram's men safely reached Bushire. The defeat at Khoshab proved not enough to force the Qajar government to surrender, the Persians continuing to mobilize and assembling their forces at Mohammareh. The Persians now numbered 28,000 men and eighty-five guns, representing – at least on paper – a formidable enemy for the British expeditionary force. Meanwhile, Britain had sent a token force up the Shatt al-Arab waterway to attack the Persian territories in southern Mesopotamia and threaten the urban centre of Basra, near Mohammareh. The Qajars were taken by surprise by this move, as well as by the outbreak of a series of local revolts in their northern territories, which were instigated by British agents.

The Persian troops deployed at Mohammareh heavily fortified their positions, using a river as a natural barrier behind which their artillery was entrenched. After most of the British expeditionary force was moved by sea to Basra, it became clear that the decisive clash of the conflict was about to take place. On 26 March 1857, the British troops attacked the fortified Persian positions, with the support of their naval artillery firing from the warships that transported the expeditionary force. The infantry commanded by Havelock could disembark practically unopposed, the steamers of the Royal Navy having silenced most of the enemy batteries. Mohammareh was taken without the British suffering any significant losses, the Persians preferring to abandon it rather than put up a stout defence. During the following days, the British transformed Mohammareh into an effective logistical base and then marched on the nearby town of Ahvaz, which was taken on 1 April. Before Outram could continue his advance across Persian Mesopotamia, however, he was informed that the hostilities with Persia had ceased since the Qajars had finally agreed to sign a peace treaty with Great Britain. According to this treaty, Herat was returned to Afghanistan and the Qajars recognized the latter country as part of the British sphere of influence in Asia. In October 1857, the British troops were evacuated from Persia but were soon in action again dealing with the Indian Mutiny, which erupted just after the end of the Anglo-Persian War.

Following the Anglo-Persian War, the Persian Empire came under increasingly strong British political and diplomatic influence, which co-existed with that established by the Russians since 1828. By the end of the 1870s, both Britain and Russia wanted to transform Afghanistan into a protectorate, but its ruler, Sher Ali, was determined to remain fully independent from the control of any foreign nation. The British, having already suffered a major defeat in Afghanistan during the First Anglo-Afghan War, were cautious in their military initiatives, but nevertheless could not permit an increasing Russian penetration into Afghanistan. Following the Congress of Berlin that took place in 1878, tensions between Britain and Russia grew considerably, the two powers having contrasting interests in various regions of the world, including the Middle East and Central Asia. In the summer of 1878, the Russians sent an uninvited diplomatic mission to Kabul, with the objective of imposing their military protection on the Afghans. Sher Ali tried to keep the Russian mission out of his country, but in the end was forced to welcome them. The British responded to the Russian initiative by demanding that Sher Ali accept a British diplomatic mission too. At this point the Afghan ruler, fearing that his country could become a battlefield between two rival empires, refused to receive any British mission. Lord Lytton, the Viceroy of India, considered the Afghan response provocative, a sign that the Russians were about to transform Afghanistan into a puppet state. In September 1878, a diplomatic mission sent from British India was turned back by the Afghans as it approached the eastern entrance of the Khyber Pass. The main route connecting India with Afghanistan, the Khyber Pass was of crucial strategic importance for both the British and the Afghans. Following the repulse of their diplomatic mission, the British decided to open hostilities against Sher Ali, heralding the outbreak of the Second Anglo-Afghan War.

In November 1878, a British invasion force of around 50,000 soldiers – most of whom were native Indian troops – attacked Afghanistan in three columns. On 21 November 1878, one of the three columns, the Peshawar Valley Field Force comprising several units made up of Sikhs, attacked strong Afghan defensive positions at the western end of the Khyber Pass. The Afghans, despite their numerical superiority, were soundly defeated at the Battle of Ali Masjid and forced to flee. This allowed the British to enter Afghan territory and march on Kabul. On 2 December 1878, the smallest of the three British invading columns fought against an Afghan force at Peiwar Kotal, a mountain pass that connected the Kuram Valley with the province of Kabul. Despite being vastly outnumbered, the British were able to obtain a clear victory over the Afghans. Following these events, the Afghans tried to come to terms with the British and asked for Russian mediation that never materialized. On 21 February 1879, Sher Ali died and his successor – Mohammad Yaqub – signed a peace agreement with the British to prevent the fall of Kabul. According to the Treaty of Gandamak, Mohammad Yaqub relinquished control of Afghan foreign affairs to Britain and a British diplomatic representative was installed in Kabul. In addition, the Afghans were to cede the Khyber Pass and various frontier areas to the British. The treaty was extremely favourable for Britain, but as soon as the British troops left Afghanistan an uprising took place in Kabul, during which the British diplomatic representative – Major Pierre-Louis Cavagnari – was assassinated together with his guards and staff. As a result of this, hostilities resumed in September 1879 and the British assembled the Kabul Field Force of 7,500 men (later increased to 14,000). On 6 October, the Kabul Field Force defeated an Afghan army at the Battle of Charasiab; two days later it occupied the Afghan capital. It seemed that the hostilities had come to an end, but in December an Afghan army made up of 50,000 irregulars laid siege to the British in Kabul, as had happened during the First Anglo-Afghan War. This time, however, the arrival of a British relief column led to the defeat of the Afghan besiegers. Mohammad Yaqub, who played a role in the organization of the siege, was forced to abdicate by the British, but hostilities continued as several Afghan tribal chiefs had no intention of surrendering. Afghan resistance was led by the governor of Herat province, Ayub Khan, who on 27 July 1880 obtained a Pyrrhic victory over a small British force at the Battle of Maiwand and started besieging the city of Kandahar. At this point of the war, the British decided to eliminate the menace represented by Ayub Khan and marched with a relief column of 10,000 men on Kandahar. On 1 September, at the decisive Battle of Kandahar, the forces of Ayub Khan were completely routed and his uprising was brought to an end. A new pro-British ruler was put on the Afghan throne, who confirmed the Treaty of Gandamak in all its components. The Second Anglo-Afghan War was over, but the Great Game between Britain and Russia would continue for several more decades.

The Anglo-Sikh Wars, 1845–1849

The Sikh Empire, the last great regional power that emerged in India before the ascendancy of Britain's colonial rule, originated in 1799 under the leadership of Maharaja Ranjit Singh. The Sikh religion emerged in the Punjab region of India around the end of the fifteenth century and gradually expanded until becoming the fifth largest religion of the world. It developed from the spiritual teachings of Guru Nanak, the first guru or master of the Sikh faith; being a monotheistic religion based on a complex system of philosophical precepts, it was soon persecuted by the Muslim rulers of the Moghul Empire who controlled most of India during the seventeenth century. The religious persecutions suffered by the Sikhs triggered them into establishing a military force to defend their expanding communities in Punjab. This force became a proper army in 1699, known as the Khalsa, at a time when the Sikhs were struggling to gain independence from the decaying Moghul Empire. By the end of the eighteenth century, with the disappearance of the Moghuls, all the Sikh autonomous communities in Punjab were unified as a single political entity under the guidance of Ranjit Singh, a great military leader, who conducted several victorious campaigns in expanding the territory of what soon became an empire. At its peak, before the outbreak of the First Anglo-Sikh War with the East India Company, the Sikh Empire extended from the Khyber Pass in the west to the borders of Tibet in the east, and from the Indus River in the south to Kashmir in the north. From their capital in Lahore, the Sikh Maharajas – having expelled the Afghans from the whole of Punjab – ruled over a vast and multi-ethnic state, which remained as the only Indian native state fully independent from British rule by the 1840s. Ranjit Singh modernized and Westernized the Sikh Army during his reign, transforming it into the most powerful native military force in India. By then known as the Dal Khalsa, it was the most dangerous enemy ever faced by the British in India.

When Ranjit Singh, nicknamed the Lion of Punjab, died in 1839, his successors did little to establish positive diplomatic relations with Britain. Within a few years, tensions started to grow between the Sikh Empire and the East India Company. The

British established a large military base at Ferozepur, near the border between British India and Sikh territory, in order to check any military moves by the Sikhs. When a large part of the company's Bengal Army was transferred to Ferozepur in late 1845, the Sikh Army was mobilized in anticipation of an imminent British invasion. Although Sikh forces did not cross the border, their mobilization was perceived as a declaration of war by the British. As a result, the First Anglo-Sikh War erupted on 11 December 1845. The main Sikh army crossed the Sutlej River and advanced against the British positions at Ferozepur, while a smaller Sikh force clashed with the bulk of the British troops that were moving against Sikh territory at the Battle of Mudki. The clash at Mudki ended in an indecisive victory for the British, who suffered heavy casualties during the engagement. The main Sikh army then encamped at Ferozeshah, establishing fortified positions. On 21 December, the British decided to attack the Sikh troops in what became known as the Battle of Ferozeshah. During a hard-earned victory for the British, they were only able to dislodge the Sikhs from their defensive positions after having been decimated by enemy artillery. The Battle of Ferozeshah showed how well-trained the Sikh Army was and how difficult it would be for the British to win the war. After the Battle of Ferozeshah, the Sikhs fell back to Aliwal on the Sutlej River, where they established a new camp and reorganized their troops while waiting for the arrival of substantial reinforcements.

On 28 January 1846, the decisive Battle of Aliwal, one of the largest clashes ever fought in India, took place between some 20,000 Sikh soldiers and 12,000 British troops. The engagement began with a successful British infantry attack, which eliminated all the advanced positions of the Sikhs, followed by a massive British cavalry charge, led by the 16th Lancers. The lancers, having routed the Sikh cavalry, continued their attack by moving against the main body of the Sikh regular infantry. This deployed into a square defensive formation and put up very strong resistance before being broken by a charge of the 16th Lancers. With the Sikh infantry also being decimated by the fire of the British artillery, the Battle of Aliwal came to an end. The Sikh retreat soon became a rout, most of their artillery being captured by the British. After the defeat of Aliwal, the Sikh leaders decided to continue their fightg against the British, reorganizing their forces in view of another pitched battle. All the military reserves of the Sikh Empire were mobilized and a new fortified camp was established at Sobraon. On 10 February, British forces, including substantial numbers of native Indian troops, attacked the Sikhs in the Battle of Sobraon. The British artillery bombarded the defensive positions of their enemy for two hours, but with little success. After the batteries ran out of ammunition, the British launched a large-scale infantry attack against the right wing of the Sikh Army. However, this attack was a failure, the Sikh infantry not only resisting but even launching various effective counter-attacks. After some intense fighting took place, with strong attacks by both sides, British engineers were finally able to open a breach in the fortifications protecting the right wing of the Sikh Army. The British infantry gained the upper hand in this sector of the line and the Sikh troops were forced to fall back. However, they had the Sutlej River at their back and just one pontoon bridge to cross it, creating a potentially very dangerous situation. Indeed, under the weight of the fleeing soldiers trying to retreat across it, the bridge collapsed and many Sikh soldiers fell into the river. Nearly 20,000 Sikh troops were trapped between the advancing British troops and the Sutlej; none of them tried to surrender, putting up a stubborn but pointless resistance that surprised their opponents. Many Sikh irregulars rushed forward from their formations to attack the British infantry with sword in hand, but were massacred by musket fire, while the British horse artillery fired into the crowds of Sikh soldiers who were swimming in the waters of the Sutlej. By the time the fighting died down, the Sikh Army had lost over 10,000 men and all its artillery.

Following its disaster at Sobraon, the Sikh Empire was forced to surrender and sign the Treaty of Lahore on 9 March 1846. Under the terms of the treaty, the East India Company annexed a large portion of Sikh territory located between the Beas and Sutlej rivers. The Sikhs also had to cede Kashmir, Hazarah and all the territory between the Beas and Indus rivers. Kashmir was later sold by the East India Company to a friendly Indian prince, the Raja of Jammu, who purchased it for 7.5 million rupees. A British resident was established in the Sikh capital of Lahore, providing the company with indirect control over the Sikh government. Following the end of hostilities, the Sikh Army was greatly reduced in numbers, which caused great discontent, and it seemed likely that some northern territories of the Sikh state could secede and join Afghanistan. The British were unwilling to incur the economic and manpower costs of using their Bengal Army to garrison Sikh territory, so did not leave any garrison in what remained of the Sikh Empire. In 1848, a major uprising took place in some of the largest urban centres that had previously been controlled by the Sikhs, which developed into a full-scale conflict, known as the Second Anglo-Sikh War. On this occasion, the British had no large Sikh regular army to face on the battlefield, but had to crush a violent rebellion involving many civilians. In 1849, after the Sikhs had obtained some initial successes, the ruler of Afghanistan – Dost Mohammad Khan – decided to join them. On 21 February 1849, however, British forces crushed Sikh troops at the Battle of Gujrat, where the Sikhs lost some 5,000 men and all their artillery, which convinced the Afghans to end their support for the Sikh cause. The Second Anglo-Sikh War was thus over, as was the glorious history of the Sikh Empire. On 29 March 1849, the whole of Punjab was annexed by the East India Company and any form of Sikh state ceased to exist.

The Indian Mutiny, 1857–1858

The Indian Mutiny broke out in 1857, the largest military uprising ever seen among the colonial troops of the British Empire. The rebellion involved a large portion of the East India Company's native forces and almost caused the total collapse of Britain's colonial presence in India. It was ignited by the diffusion of a false story related to the introduction of the new Pattern 1853 Enfield rifle, according to which the cartridges of the weapon were greased with the fat of pigs (that was unclean to Muslims) and the fat of cows (which was holy to Hindus). The sepoys of the Bengal Army, upon learning that they would be required to bite off the end of the new cartridges before loading their rifles, began fearing that the British authorities had plans to Christianize all of them and thus revolted against their white officers. The Indian Mutiny of 1857–58 was characterized by many atrocities, the sepoys soon being joined by increasing numbers of civilians who wanted to free their homeland of British control. The Indian rebels soon chose as their political and moral leader Bahadur Shah, the last exponent of the Moghul Dynasty that had ruled over India for centuries. The mutineers killed without mercy thousands of British civilians living in India and occupied the city of Delhi, with chaos and anarchy starting to spread across British India. Luckily for the British, the Madras Army and Bombay Army remained loyal to the East India Company. The British authorities could also count on the support of the elite military units recruited from the Sikhs of Punjab and the Gurkhas of Nepal. When the Indian Mutiny broke out, most of the British Army's forces were still in the process of being redeployed as the Crimean War had ended just a few months before. Nevertheless, the British took advantage of the lack of coordination that affected the mutineers and soon started to counter the rebel sepoys' activities. British troops besieged Delhi between June and September 1857, and after some harsh fighting they were able to reconquer the city and capture Bahadur Shah. Meanwhile, the rebels had obtained several important victories and forced their enemies to evacuate various strongholds (such as Cawnpore and Lucknow). During 1858, the British gradually regained control, clearing the rebels from central India and retaking most of the urban settlements that had been lost. Bands of sepoys reverted to guerrilla warfare, but one by one they were all defeated. Hundreds of rebels were captured and then executed by being blown from artillery pieces. Following the final suppression of the Indian Mutiny, on 1 November 1858, Queen Victoria took over the governing of India, which officially became part of the British Empire as a new colony.

Chapter 10

The Asian Campaigns of the British Army

The Opium Wars, 1839–1860

From the closing decades of the eighteenth century, the Qing Empire of China decided to reduce as much as possible its contacts and exchanges with the rest of the world. For an immense country like China, however, closing all ports to foreign trade soon proved impossible, the European powers being determined to continue trading with the Qing Empire. The Manchu Dynasty that dominated the Qing Empire tried to limit incoming foreign trade by confining it to the southern port city of Canton, but this proved unsuccessful. During the early nineteenth century, the demand for Chinese luxury goods – such as silk, porcelain and tea – increased significantly in Europe and created a trade imbalance between China and Great Britain. In order to eliminate the trade imbalance, which could potentially affect its financial stability, Britain began to grow opium in north-eastern India and to allow private merchants to sell it to Chinese smugglers. This illegal sale of narcotics reversed the Chinese trade surplus, drained the Qing economy of silver and increased the number of opium addicts in China. In 1839, the Manchus, having rejected proposals to legalize and tax opium, halted the opium trade completely. British opium dealers were forced to hand over 2.37 million pounds of opium, which was publicly destroyed, while all other supplies were confiscated and a blockade of foreign merchant ships was ordered. Tensions rapidly grew between China and Britain, and following various incidents, fighting broke out. The British government supported its merchants' demand for compensation for seized goods and insisted on the principles of free trade. The Royal Navy sent its modern warships to break the Chinese naval blockade and launch a naval offensive against the Qing Empire, which lasted until August 1842. The Chinese, after suffering a series of humiliating military defeats, were forced to sign the humiliating Treaty of Nanking, according to which China was obliged to increase foreign trade and provide compensation to the British merchants. Additionally, the Manchus had to cede Hong Kong to the British, who soon transformed their new possession into a flourishing commercial outpost and their main military base in China. The First Opium War marked the beginning of modern Chinese history and of what became known as the 'century of humiliation' for China.

Following the First Opium War, the Qing Empire experienced a series of famines and natural disasters that had a devastating effect on its economy. Farmers started to be heavily over-taxed, rents rose dramatically and peasants began to desert their lands in droves. The use of opium continued to be a social plague, banditry became common in rural areas and numerous secret societies emerged across China. Despite all this, the Chinese population increased rapidly during the mid-nineteenth century, but this demographic boom proved a massive problem since the amount of cultivated land remained the same. The central government did nothing to solve the many problems existing in China and became increasingly corrupt; it was particularly weak in the southern regions of the empire, where local clans represented the dominant political power. Following the progressive weakening of the Qing Empire, the British tried to expand their privileges in China by demanding that the Manchu authorities renegotiate the Treaty of Nanking. The British wanted to open all Chinese ports to international trade (the original treaty obliged the Chinese to open just five of their ports) and to legalize the opium trade. The Qing government rejected the British requests, but was in no condition to wage war due to its internal problems. As a result, following the outbreak of the Second Opium War in 1856, British troops – supported by France – obtained a series of stunning victories that culminated with their occupation of Peking. In 1860, having suffered several humiliating defeats, the Manchus were forced to open more ports to foreign trade, legalize the import of opium, permit the establishment of foreign legations in Peking and allow Christian missionary activity. In addition, the Chinese Empire had to cede to Britain the Kowloon Peninsula, which was annexed to Hong Kong.

The Boxer Rebellion, 1899–1901

During the late nineteenth century, northern China entered a period of anarchy and chaos, with villagers fearing foreign expansionism and having strong xenophobic feelings. Christian missionaries and European merchants became particular targets of the new ethnic intolerance by the Chinese. From 1899, following a series of natural disasters, including the flooding of the Yellow River, a new religious movement known as the Boxers emerged in northern China. The Boxers – whose nickname derived from them practicing ritualized martial arts – pursued anti-colonial and anti-Christian ideals. Their main objective was to restore the greatness of Qing China by destroying any form of foreign presence or influence. The religiously fanatic Boxers spread violence across northern China, attacking an increasing number of Westerners. They were backed by the Qing imperial authorities, which did nothing to halt their outrages as they considered the Boxers a useful tool with which foreigners could be expelled from China. Hundreds of foreign diplomats, missionaries and Chinese Christians took refuge in the Legation Quarter of Peking to save themselves from the fury of the Boxers, who besieged them with a massive army. The colonial powers responded by forming what was known as the Eight-Nation Alliance, which comprised Great Britain, France, Russia, Germany, Austria-Hungary, Italy, USA and Japan. An international task force was assembled to free the Legation Quarter from the Boxers, but their first attempt to reach Peking was repulsed. After the Qing government started to openly support the Boxers and declared war on the Western powers, the Eight-Nation Alliance assembled a larger expeditionary corps of some 20,000 men that defeated the imperial forces and reached Peking on 14 August 1900 to relieve the fifty-five-day siege of the legations. Thousands of Boxers were captured and executed, while Russia and Japan sent sizeable military contingents to occupy northern China. On 7 September 1901, the Qings were forced to sign the Boxer Protocol, according to which they had to pay an immense war indemnity to the westerners. Members of the alliance were permitted to deploy their own troops inside Peking, and from 1901 onwards were assigned several 'concessions' (small colonial outposts) on Chinese territory.

Chapter 11

The African Campaigns of the British Army

The Xhosa Wars, 1811–1879

The first European settlement at the Cape of Good Hope was established by the Dutch East India Company in 1652, but for a long time the new colony on the extreme southern tip of Africa remained very small. The Dutch had only gone to the Cape to establish a way-station to service their fleet on the long haul to their flourishing colonies in Asia (Indonesia), so were not interested in exploring and settling the hinterland of present-day South Africa. This region was inhabited by the most warlike peoples of Africa, notably the Xhosas, who were settled in the south-eastern part of modern South Africa. Over time, the number of Dutch colonists gradually expanded, mostly due to the arrival of religious refugees from Europe. These grew into a hardy breed who established flourishing farms thanks to the employment of black slave labour, pushing determinedly to expand into the African hinterland. The new colonists, who became known as Boers, or farmers, were forever searching for fresh hunting and grazing lands. They had a very austere and independent existence, developing their own culture and traditions. By the end of the eighteenth century, European settlement had crept steadily along the eastern seaboard of South Africa and the Boers had started fighting against the Xhosas. The Dutch East India Company fought three wars along the eastern frontier of Cape Colony during the late eighteenth and into the nineteenth century: the first in 1779–81, then from 1789–93 and finally in 1799–1803. These did not lead to any significant changes, the Boers and Dutch colonial troops proving unable to defeat the Xhosas. Having lived in eastern South Africa for a thousand years, the Xhosas were farm-working agro-pastoralists who had a semi-nomadic lifestyle. They were extremely warlike and were used to living very simply, spending much of each year crossing mountains and rivers with their cattle and goat herds in search of the best grazing grounds. Inter-tribal warfare was a fundamental component of the Xhosas' daily life, it being common for them to defend their cattle from the attacks of rival tribes as well as to conduct predatory raids and incursions against their enemies. The Xhosas were skilled at performing guerrilla operations using hit-and-run tactics and were famed as cattle raiders. They were thus not easy to defeat for the Dutch colonial troops, who were not used to fighting in the bush of South Africa. Since the beginning of their settlement in Africa, the Boers had developed their own irregular militia which was influenced by the tactics of the Xhosas and was organized into commandos, district-based military units that could be assembled very rapidly. Their members wore no uniforms, provided their own weapons, elected their own officers in a democratic way and fought as highly mobile mounted infantrymen by employing the same hit-and-run tactics as the Xhosas. The Boers also deployed their own native auxiliaries – known as Fingoes – who played a prominent role in the Xhosa Wars by acting as guides and explorers for their European masters.

In 1806, as part of the Napoleonic Wars that saw the Dutch fighting as allies of France, Britain organized a military expedition to conquer Cape Colony. By the beginning of 1806, the Dutch only had a small military garrison at Cape Colony, deploying just the following troops in South Africa: one battalion of line infantry (with one company of grenadiers and seven companies of fusiliers), one battalion of German infantry (mercenaries from Waldeck, with one company of light infantry and six companies of fusiliers), one battalion of light infantry with four companies, one independent company of auxiliary infantry, two independent companies of light infantry, one battalion of native light infantry (recruited from the Hottentot tribes and mustering four companies), one squadron of dragoons (equipped with four light field pieces), four companies of foot artillery, two companies of auxiliary artillery, one company of native artillery (recruited from Java in Indonesia and from Mozambican slaves), two infantry companies of Boers, six cavalry companies of Boers and 200 sailors/marines from the crews of two French warships beached at Cape Colony. The British expeditionary force, commanded by commodore Home Riggs Popham, was much larger and comprised the following units: 24th Regiment of Foot, 59th Regiment of Foot, 71st Regiment of Foot, 72nd Regiment of Foot, 83rd Regiment of Foot, 93rd Regiment of Foot, four troops from 20th Light Dragoons and detachments of the Royal Artillery and Royal Engineers. The British land forces were commanded by General Sir David Baird, while the Dutch defenders were under the orders of Cape Colony's governor, Willem Janssens. Soon after the arrival of the British fleet on 4 January 1806, Janssens mobilized his garrison (calling up the militia) and declared martial law. The decisive engagement between the British and Dutch took place on the slopes of Blaauwberg Mountain on 8 January. Most of the Dutch units disintegrated even before coming into contact with the enemy, except for the French sailors and marines and the Javanese artillerymen, who put up a desperate resistance that was crushed by the gallant charge of the 71st Regiment of Foot. Cape Town was occupied by the British on the following day, and although Janssens and his remaining forces continued to resist for another week they eventually capitulated.

Most of the Dutch troops were repatriated, and in 1814 Cape Colony was officially ceded by the Netherlands to Great Britain. The new British colonial authorities in South Africa reorganized the Hottentot Light Infantry inherited from the Dutch as the Cape Regiment, which mustered ten companies (with white officers and NCOs). The unit was expanded with the addition of a light cavalry troop during the Napoleonic Wars, but in 1817 most of the corps was disbanded and what remained of it was reorganized as two company-sized autonomous units tasked with protecting the north-eastern frontier of Cape Colony: Cape Light Infantry and Cape Cavalry. In 1820, these were combined together and redesignated as the Cape Corps. In 1827, its cavalry component was disbanded, while the infantry was expanded to become a battalion of mounted infantry that assumed the denomination of the Cape Mounted Riflemen. The specific task of the Cape Mounted Riflemen, who always included significant numbers of Hottentot natives, was to patrol the north-eastern frontier of Cape Colony and to deal with the frequent raiding activities of the Xhosas.

During the nineteenth century, Britain fought a total of six wars against the Xhosas, commonly known as the Cape Frontier Wars or Kaffir Wars, since they took place on the north-eastern border of Cape Colony against the Xhosas, whom most of the British called Kaffirs. The first war of 1811–12 was a small-scale affair, involving British troops clearing the area around the Fish River of the groups of Xhosa that had settled on it. This enabled the Boers to create some new communities and expand their presence along the frontier. The second war of 1818–19 began as a civil conflict between two rival factions of the Xhosas, one of which was strongly anti-British. The warriors of this group attacked the whites' settlement of Grahamstown, but were repulsed after suffering severe losses. After this success, the British pushed the Xhosas further east beyond the Fish River and created a new buffer zone that was located between that river and the Keiskamma River. During the 1820s, however, insecurity persisted along the Kaffir Frontier, the Xhosas starting to come under increasing expansionist pressure from the Zulus, who were advancing southwards from their homeland. The Xhosas, in order to continue living according to their traditional lifestyle, had no choice but to settle new lands that were already considered British-held territory. Xhosa cattle-raiders began crossing the Keiskamma River more frequently, their incursions often causing violent retaliatory raids by the Boers, who employed very harsh methods in order to pursue their own expansionist plans. On 11 December 1834, a Boer commando killed a high-ranking Xhosa chief, which caused a large-scale reaction with the Kaffirs mobilizing an army of 10,000 warriors. Sweeping across the north-eastern frontier into the territory of Cape Colony, the Kaffirs pillaged and burned many settler homesteads. The Boers living on the farms that were attacked took refuge in the settlement of Grahamstown, where they were able to resist the native raiders. The response to the Xhosas' actions was swift and effective, the Boers mobilizing their own forces and inflicting a heavy defeat on the Kaffirs in the Winterberg Mountains in the north of the region. The British sent their regular troops to Grahamstown, from where they launched a rapid retaliatory campaign. They advanced against the Xhosas, defeating them on several occasions and obliging most of the native leaders to surrender or fall back to the inhospitable Amatola Mountains. The main leader of the Kaffirs, King Hintsa, was forced to sign a peace treaty that was extremely favourable to the British, with all the country along the Cape's previous frontier – from the Keiskamma River to the Great Kei River – annexed as a British possession known as Queen Adelaide Province. This region was settled by native tribes that were loyal allies of the British, including the Fingoes. The native allies of the whites were all in search of new lands where they could settle, having been expelled from their homelands due to the steady expansionism of the Zulus. Hostilities between the British/Boers and the Xhosas came to an end on 17 September 1836. King Hintsa, having been kept as a hostage by the British for some time, tried to escape but was killed with a shot in the back of the head. Hintsa's murder angered the Xhosas for decades, leading to the outbreak of further conflict.

In the years that followed 1836, the Fingoes swiftly acquired firearms and organized mounted commandos following the example of the Boers. They became highly-respected among their white allies for their martial abilities. The Xhosas were severely weakened by events during the 1830s, losing some 175,000 head of cattle. The early 1840s saw the institution of a completely new British policy on the Kaffir Border, one aimed at establishing positive relations with the Xhosas. For example, a system of formal treaties was gradually developed in order to return any stolen cattle from either side. Boer territorial expansion into Xhosa lands was forbidden and some displaced Kaffir communities were permitted to move back to their original homelands. These new diplomatic relations, however, started to unravel after the Boers began putting pressure on the colonial authorities to allow them to resume their territorial expansion at the expense of the Xhosas. A new frontier war broke out in 1846 and proved to be the most violent conflict fought between the whites and the Kaffirs. For the first time, the Kaffirs made extensive use of firearms, and both sides employed large-scale scorched earth tactics. The Fingoes, with the help of their Boer allies, saw the war as an opportunity to gain revenge for earlier Xhosa attacks on their settlements, fighting with incredible determination and cruelty. King Sandile was the main Xhosa leader in the new frontier war, which began in March 1846 after the Kaffirs refused to surrender one of their number who had committed a murder. British regular forces suffered some initial setbacks in pursuing the Kaffirs, being ambushed in the Amatola Mountains and losing an entire wagon train of supplies. This forced the British troops to fall back, enabling large numbers of Xhosas to pour across the frontier. The Fingoes defended their villages with great courage, but several of their settlements were destroyed. A Xhosa force of 8,000 men attacked the British garrison at Fort Peddie, but was repulsed; it then attacked Grahamstown, but this assault also ended in failure. The Boer commandos conducted their own parallel war against the Xhosas, obtaining more successes than the British colonial troops: they raided the Kaffir homeland and forced the natives to sign a treaty under which a large portion of Xhosa land was to be ceded to the Boers. However, the British government did not recognize the treaty as legitimate and thus continued to fight against the Kaffirs. Following months of skirmishing and incursions, both sides were weakened and became fever-ridden. In December 1847, the Xhosas finally surrendered and agreed to cede to the British the lands between the Keiskamma and Kei rivers. The newly conquered territories were not absorbed into Cape Colony but became a crown dependency known as the British Kaffraria Colony.

Although the war of 1846–47 ended in a decisive victory for the British, it left many problems unsolved, with thousands of Xhosa refugees joining the few Kaffir communities that were still free, causing overpopulation and other hardships. In 1850, a prophet arose among the homeless Xhosas, encouraging them to revolt. Several frontier settlements of the whites were attacked, and the British were initially unable to launch an effective response. Several members of the native Kaffir Police, a paramilitary force that the colonial authorities had established to counter cattle theft, deserted and joined the insurgents. During 1851, however, the Xhosas' assaults against the colonial fortifications were all repulsed and significant British reinforcements arrived at Cape Colony. In 1853, the Xhosas who had revolted surrendered, having suffered heavy losses. Several years later, in 1877, the Kaffirs for the last time launched large-scale assaults on the whites' settlements located along the frontier. The first response to this offensive was provided by the Boers and the Fingoes, who killed many Xhosa warriors before any major frontier settlement could be destroyed. The British were not happy with how the local government of Cape Colony had handled the threat from the Xhosas, using this as a pretext to limit the self-government that just a few years before had been assigned to the white colonists of South Africa. The British ordered the disarmament of all the black inhabitants of Cape Colony, a drastic measure that also affected the loyal native allies of the whites and soon led to a renewal of the Kaffir revolt. The Xhosas successfully attacked several outposts and destroyed many farms before their opponents could organize an effective military response. When the whites eventually deployed an increasing number of troops, the Xhosas moved to the Amatola mountain range, where they began fighting with their traditional guerrilla methods. Several slow-moving British columns were ambushed by the Kaffir warriors in 1878 before the whites were finally able to gain the upper hand thanks to the building of a series of fortifications and the establishing of special task forces of mounted infantry. The war of 1877–78 ended with the complete annexation of all Xhosa lands to the British and was the last of the bloody Cape Frontier Wars.

The Anglo-Ashanti Wars, 1823–1900

At the beginning of the nineteenth century, Britain had only a few small colonial possessions in Western Africa: these were located in the Gulf of Guinea and consisted of modest footholds extending along the coastline. The British possessions included portions of present-day Gambia, Ghana (then known as the Gold Coast) and Sierra Leone. It was in the latter territory that the British had their main base of Freetown. In addition to Britain, the Netherlands and Denmark also had some colonial outposts in the Gulf of Guinea, which all worked as major bases for the slave trade until Britain decided to abolish the practise in 1807. The major regional power in Western Africa at the time was the Ashanti Empire, which had been created by the warlike Ashanti people during the course of the eighteenth century. The Ashanti dominated several tribal communities and gradually equipped their forces with modern muskets purchased from Danish merchants who were active on the coastline of Western Africa. These flintlock weapons, known as Long Dane muskets, were deadly in the hands of Ashanti warriors, who had become excellent marksmen. Thanks to their superior combat skills, the Ashanti were able to carry out a very successful expansionist policy, within a few years creating a multi-ethic empire whose wealth grew rapidly thanks to the slave trade. The Ashanti were part of the larger Akan ethnic group, which migrated into the forests of southern Ghana during the central centuries of the Middle Ages. The Ashanti Empire was the result of a long and complex political process, which saw the unification of several different clans into a loose tribal confederation. Its religious and social unity was symbolized by a sacred Golden Stool, which was believed by the Ashanti to contain the soul of their people. After the arrival of European explorers and traders in Western Africa during the early eighteenth century, the Ashanti – thanks to the wealth deriving from their gold reserves – bought large numbers of modern weapons from the whites and used them to significantly expand their territorial possessions. The Ashanti Empire traded with the Europeans in gold, ivory and slaves and developed an effective administrative and legal system.

The Ashanti could easily mobilize around 80,000 warriors by the beginning of the nineteenth century, including small cadres of regular professional soldiers which trained and led militia contingents called up by the various provincial governors. While on the march, the Ashanti fighters were usually deployed in five main groups: an advance guard, main body, right wing, left wing and rearguard. This system provided flexibility in the densely forested territories on which the Ashanti armies typically operated. The Ashanti had no cavalry, only the high-ranking officers of their army being mounted. Ashanti tactics featured ambushes and envelopment manoeuvres on the wings, while their traditional weapons included spears and bows as well as massive swords called akrafena. Prior to 1821, British territorial possessions in Western Africa were not administered directly by the Crown, but by the African Company of Merchants, a private commercial organization. This body signed a treaty of friendship with the Ashanti Empire in 1817, recognizing Ashanti claims to sovereignty over much of the Gold Coast. In 1821, the African Company of Merchants was dissolved and the British government assumed direct control over the various trading forts on the coastline of Western Africa. From 1800, to garrison these forts, the British government raised a special military corps made up of deserters and condemned servicemen. Once in Africa, the unit – originally consisting of two companies – was enlarged with the inclusion of local black recruits. In 1804, the corps received the new denomination of the Royal African Corps, six of its companies being sent to South Africa in 1817. The four companies remaining in Western Africa were reduced to a single one that continued to exist until 1840.

The First Anglo-Ashanti War began on 1 February 1823, when a group of Ashanti warriors kidnapped and murdered a black soldier of the Royal African Corps. The killing of a single man was enough to justify a rapid escalation, tension having long been growing between the Ashanti and the British. The British were commanded by the governor, Sir Charles MacCarthy, who refused to talk with the Ashanti leaders and began preparing a punitive expedition. The British had just a few hundred men in Western Africa and had very little knowledge of the interior areas inhabited by the Ashanti, who mobilized a well-disciplined force of 10,000 men, all equipped with Danish flintlock muskets. According to a contemporary observer, the Ashanti warriors marched in perfect order with their guns all carried at exactly the same angle (the only native African army of the time that was known to do so). MacCarthy made the serious mistake of dividing his weak forces into two columns and encountered the enemy on 22 January 1824, while he was at the head of just 500 soldiers. In the ensuing Battle of Nsamankow, the British were surprised by the firepower of the Ashanti, running out of ammunition and being overrun after suffering heavy losses. The Ashanti followed the defeated British in close pursuit, killing most of them, MacCarthy being shot and his skull used as a drinking cup, rimmed with gold, by the victorious Ashanti rulers. After their victory at Nsamankow, the Ashanti advanced towards the coastline, where the British tried to gather a fresh army by mobilizing their local native allies, who were traditional enemies of the Ashanti. The British built some improvised defensive positions north of Accra, where they deployed a contingent of Royal Marines and a battery of Congreve rockets, in addition to their native allies. When the Ashanti attacked the British positions frontally, it initially seemed that they were gaining the upper hand. However, the situation was turned on its head when the British fired their rockets, the Ashanti being shocked by the noise and power of a weapon that they had never seen before. The clash thus ended as a significant defeat for the Ashanti Empire. Hostilities continued – albeit with a much lesser intensity – until 1831, when the Pra River was accepted as the border between the Ashanti Empire and the British possessions.

In 1863, after three decades of peace but continual preparation for war, a large Ashanti army crossed the Pra River in search of a fugitive who wanted to place himself under the protection of the British. The British responded by mobilizing their forces to face the Ashanti, but the hostilities of this Second Anglo-Ashanti War lasted for just a few months without seeing any major clash. Both the opposing armies suffered many losses through epidemics, and the conflict ended up as a costly stalemate. In 1872, Britain expanded its territories in Western Africa by purchasing the Dutch colonial possessions in the region, which included some areas that had long been claimed by the Ashanti Empire. When the Ashanti invaded the former Dutch territories soon after learning that these had been annexed by the British, General Garnet Wolseley was sent to Western Africa at the head of an expeditionary force that numbered 2,500 men. This included single battalions from the Black Watch, the Royal Welch Fusiliers and the Rifle Brigade, a Naval Brigade made up of disembarked sailors, detachments of the Royal Artillery and Royal Engineers, elements of the Royal Marines, some auxiliary native units and the 1st and 2nd West India Regiments. The latter two corps had a very peculiar history, being strongly linked to that of the British colonial possessions in Western Africa. Until 1795, the British military garrison of the West Indies was entirely made up of white regular regiments, which were sent to the Caribbean for periods of service before being transferred to other areas of the British Empire. However, the white soldiers disliked service in the West Indies as its tropical climate was very unhealthy and fevers killed dozens of them every year. To solve this problem, since 1795, the British military had started raising native regiments made up of black individuals from the Caribbean colonies. Known as West India Regiments, these units had white officers and NCOs, performing extremely well against both external and internal enemies, including the maroons, runaway slaves who often attacked the lucrative colonial plantations. From 1812, the West India Regiments – which were reduced to two in 1819 – started to have a recruiting station in Western Africa, and since 1818 they had been tasked with providing military contingents that could operate in the British colonies of Western Africa. The unhealthy tropical climate of this region was very similar to that of the Caribbean islands, being deemed unsustainable for Britain's white soldiers.

The military expedition led by Wolseley was covered by several war correspondents, including the famous Henry Morton Stanley (of 'Dr Livingstone, I presume?' fame). Although hostilities in the Third Anglo-Ashanti War began in 1873, the bulk of the British troops arrived in Western Africa only in January 1874. Before the landing of the infantry units, the Royal Engineers started building a road to connect Cape Coast Castle with Coomassie, some 160 miles long and suitable for troop movements. The task was a massive challenge for the Royal Engineers. At the end of each day's march, roughly every 10 miles, the engineers built a fortified camp consisting of 70ft-long huts inside a stockade. Clearing large areas of trees and undergrowth proved particularly difficult for the Royal Engineers due to the tropical climate and wild animals. They also had to build a total of 273 bridges of various dimensions, as well as towers designed for observation and offices for a new telegraphic line. Tropical diseases, despite the use of quinine, killed many white soldiers, but by 29 January 1874, the road had reached the enemy positions and Wolseley could count on an effective supply line. Two days later, the British attacked the Ashanti positions in the village of Amoaful. The Black Watch charged frontally with bayonets, with fire support from the Rifle Brigade, while the other British troops encircled the enemy positions. The Battle of Amoaful was a disastrous defeat for the Ashanti, since it opened to Wolseley the way to Kumasi, the capital of the Ashanti Empire. Kumasi was occupied by the British on 4 February, Wolseley ordering the demolition with explosives of the town, including the impressive royal palace. Thereafter, the Ashanti continued their resistance for a few months, using guerrilla tactics, until they were finally forced to surrender. In July 1874, the war came to an end with the signing of the Treaty of Fomena, the Ashanti agreeing to pay a large indemnity and to renounce all their expansionist ambitions. Wolseley had been able to successfully complete the campaign in just a few months, before the onset of the unhealthy season, for which he earned promotion and was showered with military honours. This very capable general learned a lot from his campaign in Western Africa and was the first senior officer of the British Army to introduce a new uniform specifically designed for field use in a tropical climate (including the famous Wolseley pith helmet).

In 1891, having come under increasingly strong British political influence, the Ashanti Empire turned down an unofficial offer to become a British protectorate. This was perceived as a hostile move by the British, who were worried that the Ashanti lands might be invaded by their French or German colonial rivals, who both had strong interests in Western Africa. The Ashanti lands were attractive to the British Empire as they were rich in gold, cocoa and rubber. As a consequence, in December 1895, a British expeditionary force invaded the Ashanti Empire and reached Kumasi within a few weeks. On this occasion the Ashanti did not put up a strong resistance, the Fourth Anglo-Ashanti War coming to a successful conclusion for the British very rapidly. The Ashanti leaders were forced to sign a treaty that transformed their empire into a British protectorate before being sent into exile in the Seychelles. One of the most senior British officers during this conflict was Major Robert Baden-Powell (later the founder of the Scout Movement), who published a detailed diary about it. In 1898, the British started building a railroad that connected the coastline with Kumasi, at the same time beginning to directly control Ashanti political life. This caused increasing resentment in a warlike society that had long dominated the other native peoples of Western Africa. On 25 March 1900, the British representative in Kumasi, Sir Frederick Mitchell Hodgson, offended the most important Ashanti political and religious leaders by insisting he should sit on the sacred Golden Stool. Hodgson had not understood the importance of this symbol for the Ashanti, who considered the request of the British representative a terrible offence and thus rose up in revolt, attacking the British garrison in Kumasi to instigate the Fifth Anglo-Ashanti War (also known as the War of the Golden Stool). The British troops retreated to a small stockade that had firing turrets at each corner, where they had placed six small-calibre field guns and four Maxim machine guns. The British forces, mostly consisting of Nigerian colonial soldiers, were besieged for several weeks by 12,000 Ashanti warriors and experienced some terrible hardships until they were saved by a relief force of 1,000 men. The column arrived on 14 July, whereafter it rapidly defeated the besiegers despite having been attacked several times before reaching Kumasi. The conflict of 1900 was the last to take place between Britain and the Ashanti Empire. Upon its conclusion, all Ashanti territories were made part of the Gold Coast colony on 1 January 1902. The Ashanti, however, received the promise that their sacred Golden Stool would never again be violated.

The Abyssinian Expedition, 1867–1868

By the beginning of the 1860s, Abyssinia was undoubtedly the most important and powerful nation of Eastern Africa. The country today known as Ethiopia had a solid military reputation and was the dominant regional power in the Horn of Africa. The Abyssinian population, despite being made up of several different ethnic groups with different traditions and dress, was characterized by a common culture and a common religion that made it different from all the other peoples of Africa. For the Abyssinians were Orthodox Christians, living in an area of the world that was dominated by the Islamic faith. Furthermore, their rulers claimed to be the direct heirs of the biblical Jewish king Solomon. Over the centuries, aided by the many conflicts fought against Muslim invaders, the Abyssinians developed a strong sense of national pride, mostly aimed at the defence of their Christian faith. They became extremely warlike and started to organize their society in a militaristic manner. Abyssinia was a large realm ruled by an emperor, or negus, who could exert unlimited power over all his subjects. In practice, however, the Abyssinian monarchs had to deal with a strong feudal nobility made up of landowners. Each Abyssinian aristocrat, or ras, was a warlord: he controlled a large portion of territory and could mobilize significant numbers of warriors who were extremely loyal to him. The regional warlords were usually interested in preserving the power of the emperor when he was a capable one, but on several occasions they revolted against the negus because of their personal ambition. Indeed, it was not uncommon to see a ras initiating a civil war in order to have himself crowned emperor. No central standing army existed in Abyssinia, so the emperor could only assemble a sizeable military force through the support of his feudal lords. By the nineteenth century, the Abyssinian monarchy had become increasingly weak and civil wars started to be more frequent. The autonomy of each aristocrat became significantly larger and the military forces of the regional warlords were gradually re-equipped with modern firearms imported from abroad, replacing the traditional semi-medieval weapons previously in use.

After several decades of political anarchy, commonly known in present-day Ethiopia as the Era of the Princes, Abyssinia started to be ruled by a young and very ambitious emperor, Tewodros II. He became emperor in 1855 and tried to transform his country into a centralized monarchy with efficient institutions that was capable of countering the emerging colonial ambitions of the European powers in the Horn of Africa. Tewodros rapidly reduced the political autonomy of the regional warlords and forced them to recognize his authority. He crushed every form of internal opposition using harshly repressive methods, which significantly reduced his initial popularity. Over time, Tewodros' position as supreme ruler of Abyssinia became increasingly precarious. Most of the nobles who had been recently submitted rose up in revolt and he lost control over the peripheral areas of his nation. Tewodros' power remained strong only in the region of Lake Tana, where he had his main fortified stronghold of Magdala. Abyssinia was shattered by violent civil conflicts for several years, but the emperor also had to face the expansionist ambitions of his external enemies: the Egyptians, in particular, were interested in expanding southwards across Sudan towards Abyssinia and dominating the western coastline of the Red Sea. Finding in a very difficult situation, Tewodros was left with little option but to ask for help from some of the leading colonial powers – including Britain – hoping that they would support the Abyssinian Christians against their Muslim enemies. However, no European nation responded to his request for help, Tewodros interpreting this lack of response as a personal snub.

The first European to cross Tewodros' path after the events described above was a British missionary named Henry Stern, who was arrested by the Abyssinians for having offended the negus in a book that he had published some time before. The book was clearly only used by Tewodros as a pretext, as he wanted European hostages in order to exert stronger diplomatic pressure on the colonial powers. Stern had mentioned in his writings the humble origins of Tewodros, which was potentially dangerous for the emperor, who had always presented himself as a legitimate member of the noble Solomonic Dynasty that had ruled Abyssinia for centuries. The arrest of Stern merely worsened relations between Britain and Tewodros, which led to the taking of more British hostages by the Abyssinians. These included the British consul in Abyssinia, Charles Duncan Cameron, who was seized along with his staff and put in chains in January 1864. The new anti-Western and anti-white policy of Tewodros was soon perceived as a serious threat by the British government, which tried to protect its citizens living in Abyssinia. In June 1866, after the failure of long and complex diplomatic negotiations, the Abyssinian monarch refused to give up his British hostages, moving them to his fortress at Magdala. A few months later, on 21 August 1867, Queen Victoria announced that a punitive military expedition would be sent against Tewodros. The task of organizing an invasion force to land in Eastern Africa was assigned to Britain's Indian colonial troops, in particular those belonging to the Bombay Army. Colonial forces in India were still at this time structured on three autonomous armies that operated independently from each other: those of Bombay, Madras Army and Bengal. The expeditionary force was commanded by General Sir Robert Napier, an experienced officer of the Royal Engineers. The appointment of Napier, who had specific technical skills, was not a casual one: Abyssinia had not been invaded for centuries due to the savage nature of its terrain, so engineering skills would be fundamental in obtaining a successful outcome to the forthcoming campaign. Preparations for the expedition were meticulous: forty-four trained elephants were sent from India to transport the heavier guns, large numbers of camels and mules were bought to transport lighter materials and it was also decided to build a railway – complete with locomotives and 20 miles of track – along the coastal plain of eastern Abyssinia in order to move troops more rapidly from the landing places. The expeditionary force assembled to campaign against Tewodros consisted of some 13,000 soldiers and included the following units:

British: 4th Regiment of Foot, 33rd Regiment of Foot, six companies from the 45th Regiment of Foot, 3rd Dragoon Guards, one battery equipped with Armstrong rifled breech-loading guns provided by the Royal Artillery, one battery with rockets provided by the Royal Navy and several officers of the Royal Engineers.

Indian: 2nd Bombay Native Infantry, 3rd Bombay Native Infantry, 10th Bombay Native Infantry, 21st Bombay Native Infantry, 25th Bombay Native Infantry, 1st Belooch Native Infantry (Bombay Army), 21st Punjab Native Infantry (Bengal Army), 23rd Punjab Native Infantry (Bengal Army, a unit of pioneers), 3rd Regiment of Bombay Native Cavalry, 10th Regiment of Bengal Native Cavalry, 12th Regiment of Bengal Native Cavalry, 1st Company of Bombay Native Artillery, detachments of the Corps of Bombay Sappers and Miners and the Corps of Madras Sappers and Miners.

The British and Indian troops were supported by more than 26,000 camp followers and had over 40,000 animals with them to transport supplies across an arid and hostile natural environment that was a logistical nightmare as the rocky terrain of Abyssinia offered little or no food resources for any foreign invader. The expedition was followed by several journalists and photographers, including Henry Morton Stanley. A total of 280 ships were needed to transport all the troops from Bombay to the coast of Abyssinia, where the invasion force landed at Zula in mid-October 1867. Zula was soon transformed into a port by the British, who quickly started penetrating inland by building the planned railroad as well as several new roads. It took the invasion force three months to trek over 400 miles of mountainous terrain from Zula to the foot of Tewodros' stronghold at Magdala. However, Napier allied himself with the various regional warlords who were in revolt against their emperor, and thus met no resistance during his advance. The support of the Abyssinian rebels was absolutely fundamental for the British, who were supplied with large amounts of food and water by the emperor's internal enemies. These were led by Dajamach Kassai, a young and capable leader who would later become emperor under the name of Yohannes IV.

When the British and Indian troops landed in Abyssinia, Tewodros was abandoned by most of his followers and his army suffered from frequent defections. When the invading force reached the territory that was under his direct control, the negus had just 10,000 warriors still under his command. Napier intelligently presented himself as a liberator for the Abyssinian nation, taking advantage of the fact that many natives considered Tewodros a despot who must be deposed as soon as possible. The friendly behaviour of the British and Indian soldiers assisted in the collaboration of Napier with the warlords who opposed Tewodros: the invading troops, for example, paid for all the food supplies they received from the local communities and did not commit any crimes during their long march. The Abyssinian emperor, being badly outnumbered, moved with all his remaining supporters and his small force of artillery to the fortress of Magdala, where he intended to resist for as long as possible, hoping that the support of his internal enemies for the foreigners would melt away when they saw the strong resistance that was being maintained. However, during his march on Magdala, the Abyssinian monarch lost many of his men, who deserted or were killed along the way by groups of local warriors who rose up in rebellion. On 9 April 1868, Napier's army reached Magdala and clashed with the emperor's forces, which had encamped in the hillsides around the fortress with around thirty artillery pieces. Tewodros, instead of defending his positions, made the fatal mistake of ordering a general attack against the British. Thousands of Abyssinian warriors – mostly armed with only spears and swords – charged the enemy lines with great courage but were annihilated by the superior firepower of Napier's men. The rockets employed by the British, as well as the Armstrong guns, killed or wounded hundreds of Abyssinian warriors.

After repelling the unexpected Abyssinian attack, the British and Indian troops prepared for the siege of the fortress of Magdala. Tewodros, realizing that he had no chance of victory, tried to open diplomatic negotiations with Napier and released two hostages. By now, however, the British wanted his unconditional surrender and it was not possible to come to terms. After all the British hostages had been released, the siege proper began: Napier's artillery bombarded the enemy positions with rockets and mortars, while elements of the Royal Engineers blew up the gates of Magdala. The British and Indian infantrymen poured into the stronghold, killing at bayonet point any remaining defenders they encountered. The Abyssinian emperor, in order to avoid capture, committed suicide by pistol shot before the British could reach him. Upon learning of their leader's death, the Abyssinian warriors ceased fighting and surrendered. The short siege of Magdala, which had been little more than a bombardment followed by a frontal assault, was a prestigious victory for Britain, being obtained for very modest casualties (just fifteen men were wounded). Following the fall of Magdala, all thirty artillery pieces of Tewodros – most of which had been produced by enslaved foreigners by very rudimental methods – were destroyed. The Abyssinian fortress was looted and burned to the ground as a punitive measure. Many historical and religious artefacts of great significance in Abyssinian culture were taken back to Britain, where they can still be seen today in the British Museum and British Library. Napier, having achieved all his objectives, returned with his troops to Zula. Dajamach

Kassai was rewarded by the British for his services with a large quantity of supplies and weapons, including six mortars, six howitzers and around 900 muskets or rifles. These military supplies would play a decisive role during subsequent Abyssinian civil wars, which resulted in the ascendancy of Dajamach Kassai as negus.

When the expeditionary force left Eastern Africa in June 1868, one British participant in the campaign – John Kirkham – decided to remain in Abyssinia as a military instructor and trained the troops of the future Yohannes IV according to contemporary European standards. Kirkham was a typical adventurer of the Victorian Age: he and his Western-drilled soldiers (known as the Emperor's Disciplined Force) played a prominent role in the civil wars that ended with the triumph of Yohannes IV and in the Ethiopian-Egyptian War of 1874–76. Against all odds, the war with Egypt ended in a decisive victory for Abyssinia, guaranteeing the country continued independence in the years immediately preceding the Scramble for Africa, the colonization of much of the continent by Western European powers. Conversely, for Egypt, the conflict of 1874–76 was a costly failure that severely hampered the expansionist ambitions of the Egyptians, leading, just five years later, to the transformation of Egypt into a British protectorate. Kirkham died in 1876, six months after having been captured by the Egyptians. Yohannes IV ruled as emperor of Abyssinia from 1871–89 and is still remembered as one of the greatest monarchs in the history of Ethiopia, having also defeated an attempted Italian invasion of his country at the Battle of Dogali in 1887. Although the 1867–68 expedition commanded by Napier was a secondary colonial campaign for Britain, it proved a real turning point in the history of present-day Ethiopia.

The Anglo-Zulu War, 1879

After Cape Colony came under British control in 1806, most of the Boers soon felt that the new British administration was unsympathetic to their needs, especially after it tried to outlaw slavery, which was the basis of the Boers' rural economy. In 1835, the Boers commissioned reconnaissance parties to travel beyond the boundaries of Cape Colony in search of lands that might be opened up for white settlement, away from British control. Between 1836 and 1840, around 6,000 Boers packed their belongings into their ox-wagons and migrated into the interior of South Africa in what became known as the Great Trek. These Boers were organized into groups linked by family ties and led by ambitious leaders. Their migration provoked decades of conflict with the native African groups they encountered along the way, causing many difficulties for the British colonial authorities. The most dangerous native enemies of the Boers were the Zulus, the most warlike people of South Africa. Under the leadership of

King Shaka, who ruled from 1816–28, the Zulus had significantly expanded the boundaries of their homeland thanks to the superior fighting ability of their military forces, which were given a new and effective organization by Shaka. The Great Trek led to the formation of several new Boer autonomous states on the north-eastern border of South Africa, which struggled against the local native communities to expand their territories. The Boers were jealous of their independence, their newly formed political entities being republics that did not recognize the suzerainty of the British Crown. In 1839, after gaining a significant victory over the Zulus at the Battle of Blood River, they established the Natalia Republic on the territory of present-day Natal. Initially, the British authorities did very little to exert their control over the new Boer state, but when it came into contact with Dutch representatives they decided to act in order to prevent the transformation of Natal into a colony of the Netherlands. The British expeditionary force occupied the Natalia Republic during 1842, having defeated the local Boer forces. Two years later, Natal was annexed to the Cape Colony, remaining so until being organized as an autonomous colony in 1854. Most of the Boers who had created the Natalia Republic did not accept becoming British subjects, trekking over the mountains that marked the new north-eastern border of the Cape Colony. In a period of about ten years, they settled over a vast territory extending north of the Orange River. In 1852, the British government signed the Sand River Convention with the 40,000 Boer people living north-east of the Cape Colony. According to this agreement, the lands located between the Orange River in the south and the Vaal River in the north were to be organized as an autonomous Boer state placed under British suzerainty; the Boer lands north of the Vaal River, instead, would be completely independent from British rule. The southern Boer state became known as the Orange Free State in 1854, while the northern one assumed the denomination of the Transvaal Republic. By signing the Sand River Convention, the British hoped to create a buffer zone in the form of the Orange Free State between their colonial possessions and the independent Boer lands. The Boers continued expanding their territories, which was always going to cause a major conflict with the Zulus, something that the British wanted to avoid. The Orange Free State was often hostile to British indirect rule and thus supported the Transvaal Republic, with the result that British plans did not work out as expected.

In January 1879, in order to solve once and for all the border disputes between the Boers and the Zulus, the British invaded Zululand with a sizeable expeditionary force. The commanders of the invasion, however, made a series of mistakes, dividing their troops into too many columns. As a result, on 22 January 1879, two British columns with 1,800 men were annihilated by 20,000 Zulu warriors at the Battle of Isandlwana. This was the worst defeat ever suffered by the British Army during its colonial campaigns, with around 1,300 men being killed. While the Battle of Isandlwana took place, another 4,000 Zulu warriors attacked a small British garrison at the border post of Rorke's Drift, where, differently from what happened at Isandlwana, the Zulus were defeated by the superior firepower of the British and were driven off after 10 hours of ferocious combat. The remaining British troops were forced to halt their advance and be reorganized following the disaster of Isandlwana. They were attacked again by the Zulus at the Battle of Kambula on 29 March, but this time the British were able to prevail. In the summer of 1879 a second invasion of Zululand was launched, which proved far more successful. The Zulus were crushed in the decisive Battle of Ulundi on 4 July, marking the end of the bloody Anglo-Zulu War and forcing the Zulu nation to accept the military supremacy of the British. The Zulu realm was divided into a series of petty kingdoms, which were officially absorbed into the British colony of Natal during 1897.

The Boer Wars, 1880–1902

Following the Anglo-Zulu War of 1879, the British tried to stabilize their colonial presence in the frontier areas of South Africa by exerting more direct control over the two Boer states. In 1877, Britain had formally annexed Transvaal to its dominions, which caused great anger among the Boers, who feared the consolidation of British presence in Natal after the Anglo-Zulu War could greatly damage their interests. On 20 December 1880, the Boers rose up in revolt and attacked a column of the 94th Regiment of Foot that was on the march. The Republic of Transvaal reaffirmed its independence from British rule and hostilities of what became known as the First Boer War began. A few days after the first clash, Boer commandos – which had all been mobilized – started besieging isolated British garrisons deployed around Transvaal. The Boers attacked the British by using hit-and-run guerrilla tactics and organizing frequent ambushes. The British regulars, dressed in their red uniforms and being unprepared to fight on a territory of which they had limited knowledge, suffered heavy losses, being unable to effectively deal with their enemies. The six British forts in Transvaal were all besieged by significant Boer forces, who did not attempt to storm the defensive positions but waged a war of attrition that caused no losses to themselves. Sniping from the hills that surrounded the forts, the commandos killed many British soldiers. The defenders of the forts, being isolated in hostile territory, looked set to run out of supplies if the British authorities did not send a relief column to Transvaal. General George Colley, governor of both Natal and Transvaal, acted rapidly in a bid to save the besieged British troops, assembling a relief column – known as the Natal Field Force – of 1,400 men near the Transvaal border. The Natal Field Force moved to a strategic pass located in the hills on the Natal–Transvaal border, known as Laing's Nek. Here, on 28 January 1881, the British tried to break through the Boers' defensive positions. However, Colley's men were repulsed with heavy losses by the commandos, which were led by the experienced Piet Joubert. Of the 480 British soldiers who attacked at Laing's Nek, around 150 were lost, including many senior officers, favoured targets of the Boer snipers. After this defeat, Colley moved south to Mount Prospect and established his main operational base there while awaiting reinforcements. The Boers started to conduct a series of rapid attacks against the British supply line that crossed Natal in order to isolate the Natal Field Force. Colley responded by organizing a convoy with a strong escort and guiding it personally towards Natal in order to restore his line of communication. On 7 February 1881, however, the British convoy was ambushed by the Joubert's Boers at the Ingogo River crossing: half of the escort – around 140 men – were killed, the commandos securing another significant victory without suffering major losses. A few days after the Battle of Ingogo, Colley finally received reinforcements from the south, including elements of the 92nd Regiment of Foot (the Gordon Highlanders) and the 83rd Regiment of Foot, under the command of Sir Evelyn Wood. Peace talks were then held and hostilities were temporarily suspended, but Colley was convinced that with the arrival of the reinforcements he could easily crush the Boers and thus decided to attack the enemy positions without waiting for the end of the discussions. Under cover of night on 26 February, British troops reached the top of Majuba Hill, which overlooked the main Boer positions. The commandos attacked the hill by using dead ground to their advantage. Shooting accurately and by using all available natural cover, they advanced rapidly to storm the top of Majuba Hill. The British soldiers, having been driven off from their positions, panicked and fled down the hill. Many of them were killed during the ensuing rout, including General Colley, who was shot in the head while attempting to rally his men. The Battle of Majuba was one of the greatest military humiliations ever suffered by the British Army, the Boers suffering practically no casualties.

Soon after the Battle of Majuba, a truce was signed; the British government, unwilling to get bogged down in a distant colonial war that would have been long and costly, agreed to sign an armistice on 6 March, which was followed by a peace treaty. According to this treaty, known as the Pretoria Convention, Transvaal regained its former autonomy and was assigned full self-government. British troops withdrew from Boer lands and peace was restored, but this situation was only temporary as discord remained between the two parties. Indeed, it was not long before the Second Boer War broke out between Britain and the Boer states in October 1899. Following the discovery of large deposits of gold on land inhabited by the Boers, thousands of

British settlers from Cape Town moved to the Transvaal Republic and Orange Free State, where they were not welcomed by the Boer communities. The British, seeking to take control of the newly found gold, reopened hostilities with the Boers. The new conflict lasted until 1902 and began with a series of striking victories for the Boers, but the British responded by sending massive reinforcements to South Africa and invading the Boer states with an army of 180,000 men. In 1900, both the Transvaal Republic and Orange Free State were annexed to the British Empire, but the Boers mounted strong resistance. They attacked the British using their usual hit-and-run guerrilla tactics setting ambushes. For two years, the British regulars – by now clad in khaki – faced the Boer commandos, suffering heavy casualties until the employment of very harsh repressive methods – which included the building of concentration camps and the use of a scorched earth policy – finally resulted in the success of the British counter-insurgence.

The Anglo-Egyptian War, 1882

The political process that led to the transformation of Egypt from a semi-autonomous vassal state of the Ottoman Empire to a British protectorate was a quite rapid one. In 1881, an ambitious officer of the Egyptian army, Arabi Pasha, mutinied against his country's central government and mounted a coup against the ruling Khedive, or governor, Tewfik Pasha. Arabi Pasha considered the Egyptian government too weak to resist the expansionist ambitions of Britain and France, and also had deep anti-European and anti-Christian feelings. During the civil war that followed the uprising of Arabi Pasha, both Britain and France supported the Khedive, over whom they exerted strong diplomatic influence. Fearing that their citizens living in Egypt could be killed or injured by Arabi Pasha's troops, the two European powers sent warships off the coast of Alexandria on 20 May 1882. A few weeks later, an anti-Christian riot took place in the port city, which resulted in the death of fifty European civilians. At this point, Britain decided to intervene in the Egyptian civil war, seeking to defeat Arabi Pasha and transform Egypt into a protectorate; the French, who would have benefited very little from an invasion of Egypt, did not follow the British in their military plans. The opening of the strategically important Suez Canal in 1869 had transformed Egypt into the most important African country, especially from Britain's point of view. The British were determined to use the Suez Canal to connect more rapidly and effectively with their vast colonial possessions in India. They had invested substantial sums of money in Egypt during the 1870s, and were consequently much troubled by the country's state of anarchy due to the ongoing civil war. On 11 July 1882, the British fleet started bombarding the city of Alexandria, which had been heavily fortified by Arabi Pasha during previous weeks. The British fleet kept up its fire on Alexandria for several days, seeking to demolish the Egyptian defensive positions. Indeed, much of the city was destroyed. The explosive shells employed by the British started fires in several areas of Alexandria. Hundreds of civilians died, especially once the Egyptian troops left the city. Alexandria was then occupied by a force disembarking from the British ships, which restored order in the city after some hours of unrest that saw lootings and violence dominating the streets.

Despite having lost Alexandria, Arabi Pasha continued his resistance by recruiting more troops. He could count on the unconditioned support of the Egyptian population and controlled most of Egypt's regular forces. The British launched a probing attack against Egyptian positions at Kafr El Dawwar to see if it was possible for them to rapidly reach Cairo, but they soon found that the Egyptian defences were too strong. As a result, in August 1882, the British government decided to assemble a large expeditionary force to invade the Suez Canal area. This comprised some 40,000 soldiers and was commanded by General Wolseley. On 5 August, having landed in Alexandria, the British force attacked the Egyptian lines at Kafr El Dawwar. The British were forced to fall back again after a probing attack, realizing that a major assault was needed to defeat the Egyptian troops deployed in the area. The original British plan to reaching Cairo from Alexandria had to be abandoned. At this point of the campaign, Wolseley decided to use the Suez Canal to outflank the Egyptian defensive positions. On 20 August, British troops that had been transported down the Suez Canal disembarked at Ismailia, which they occupied without encountering any resistance. A few days later, on 26 August, the British force met the enemy at the Kassassin lock, where, despite being outnumbered by Arabi Pasha's men, they repulsed all their assaults and forced the Egyptians to fall back with heavy losses. The whole British expeditionary force then moved to Kassassin, where it prepared for a large-scale pitched battle against the Egyptians. Arabi Pasha, determined to defend his capital of Cairo from the British, dug in his main force at Tell El Kebir, north of the railway and canal that linked Ismailia with Cairo. The Egyptian army deployed at Tell El Kebir consisted of 18,000 soldiers equipped with modern rifles and sixty pieces of artillery. Consequently, in a defensive battle, it had good chances of stopping the British assaults. Wolseley, having determined that the Egyptians had no outposts in front of their positions during the night, saw that it was possible for an attacking force to sneak up on the enemy defences under cover of darkness. The British troops duly approached the Egyptian positions by night and attacked frontally at dawn on 13 September. They did not achieve the desired surprise, however, as the infantry and artillery defending the Egyptian redoubts opened fire when the British were still 550 metres from the defences. Nevertheless, the Egyptian fire was not particularly effective and was unable to halt the advance of the British. Despite suffering some losses, the British troops attacked the enemy redoubts and seized them after a short but violent hand-to-hand fight. The Egyptians lost around 2,000 men and were completely routed. Soon after the battle, the British troops captured Cairo without meeting any serious resistance, the Egyptian capital having been left virtually undefended. With the defeat of Arabi Pasha, who fled into exile, the ruling Khedive was formally restored by the British and Egypt was transformed into a protectorate of Great Britain. Thanks to their success, Britain had direct control of the Suez Canal and was able, with Egyptian support, to colonize the vast region of Sudan.

The Mahdist War, 1881–1899

From 1880, Sudan was ruled by Charles George Gordon, an experienced British general who had been chosen by the Egyptian government as the governor of its Sudanese territories. Gordon strove to stabilize the Egyptian presence in Sudan and to counter the illegal activities of the local slave-traders, but could not prevent the ascendancy of the Mahdist State of Sudan. Ruled by a charismatic religious leader named Muhammad Ahmad, the Mahdists wanted to restore the original purity of Islam in Sudan by expelling the Egyptians. In 1881, Muhammad Ahmad proclaimed himself the Mahdi (the expected one) and launched a holy war against the foreigners living in Sudan. His religious fundamentalism soon transformed Sudanese society and caused serious trouble for the Egyptian authorities: the small Egyptian garrisons in Sudan were all destroyed by the Mahdists, except for the major one at Khartoum, the Sudanese capital, which was located on the Nile. To reconquer Sudan and deal with the Mahdists, the Egyptian government assembled an expeditionary force commanded by the British Colonel William Hicks, who held the rank of general in the Egyptian army. However, having marched without water through the Sudanese desert for several days, the column was ambushed and completely destroyed by the Mahdist insurgents in November 1883. By early 1884, the Egyptian military situation in Sudan was desperate, the Mahdists having conquered the whole country except for the city of Khartoum, where the Egyptian garrison was besieged. General Gordon repulsed several Mahdist attacks against his positions, improving the fortifications of Khartoum and obtaining some minor successes. Nevertheless, it became apparent that his remaining troops would be destroyed if no relief expedition was sent from Egypt. Since Gordon was an extremely popular figure in his homeland, and Egypt could not afford to lose Sudan, the British government finally decided to assemble a relief force to save the Sudanese capital and General Gordon from being captured by the Islamist insurgents. The Nile Expedition, which was commanded by the experienced General Garnet Wolseley, tried to reach Khartoum via the Nile River. The relief force comprised just 5,400 British soldiers, who advanced quite slowly on the Nile, having to repel several attacks by the Mahdists. Progress was also hampered by the British boats often having to be pulled through rapids by rope from the shore. Realizing that time was running out for General Gordon and his men, Wolseley split his force into two columns, sending 2,400 men mounted on dromedaries on a 280km shortcut across the desert in order to reach Khartoum sooner. Despite Wolseley's efforts, however, the Sudanese capital fell to the besieging Mahdist army of 50,000 warriors on 26 January 1885. The entire Egyptian garrison of the city was massacred, including General Gordon. Two days later, two British steamers of the relief fleet moving along the Nile reached Khartoum, but their crews soon saw that the city had fallen. The campaign continued for several more weeks, during which the British land forces moving towards the city were attacked several times by the Mahdists. Badly outnumbered, the British troops also lacked the supplies to continue campaigning in Sudan so a general retreat was ordered towards Egypt. Following his great victories, the Mahdi was able to establish an Islamic state governed by Sharia religious law in Sudan. Although he died just six months later, the Mahdist State survived him.

In 1896, the British government finally decided to support Egyptian attempts aimed at the reconquest of Sudan. General Herbert Kitchener was appointed overall commander of the Anglo-Egyptian forces for the invasion of Sudan, which began in March 1896 with Kitchener's troops entering the territory of the Mahdist State. The Anglo-Egyptian expeditionary force consisted of 11,000 soldiers and was supported by a flotilla of gunboats moving on the Nile. Kitchener's advance was slow and methodical, the Anglo-Egyptian force building fortified camps along their route of march as well as narrow-gauge railways. Except for some occasional skirmishing, the early months of the war saw no major fighting. The first serious clash was at Farka and was a serious defeat for the Mahdists, who lost around 800 warriors. Kitchener's forces invested the important settlement of Dongola, which was defended by a substantial Mahdist garrison; this was taken in September, although Kitchener's men suffered severe losses due to an outbreak of cholera in their camp. Following the fall of Dongola, the Mahdist capital of Omdurman started to be menaced by the advancing Anglo-Egyptian forces. The Mahdists then gathered all their warriors (more than 150,000 men) for a decisive pitched battle against the invaders. In January 1898, after receiving significant reinforcements from Britain and Egypt, Kitchener's troops attacked and defeated a minor Mahdist force at the Battle of Atbara. By the late summer of 1898, the Anglo-Egyptian expeditionary force mustered 26,000 soldiers assembled into two British brigades and four Egyptian brigades. On 2 September, the Battle of Omdurman was fought between the Anglo-Egyptian troops and the Mahdist army of some 52,000 warriors. However, the Mahdists were seriously outgunned by the strong artillery component of Kitchener's force. The clash began in the early morning with a massive assault by the Mahdists, who suffered severe losses during their advance, mostly caused by the fifty-two quick-firing guns of the Anglo-Egyptian artillery. After more than 4,000 Mahdists had been killed, the Anglo-Egyptian cavalry – mounted on horses and camels – came under attack from an elite force of 15,000 Mahdist warriors, but the assault was repulsed with heavy losses thanks to the accurate fire from two of the gunboats operating on the nearby Nile. After the failure of this second assault, most of the Mahdist army was routed and Kitchener ordered an advance on Omdurman. The British 21st Lancers were sent ahead to clear the plain in front of the Mahdist capital, the 400 British lancers defeat a force of 2,500 Mahdist fighters in what is considered as the last great charge in the glorious history of the British cavalry. The Mahdists then mounted a final desperate counter-attack, but this was annihilated by the quick fire of the Anglo-Egyptian Maxim machine guns. When the Battle of Omdurman was over, more than 11,000 Mahdist soldiers lay dead, and the Mahdist capital was soon occupied by Kitchener. The Anglo-Egyptian campaign lasted for several more months, during which the surviving bands of Mahdists still active in southern Sudan were crushed. By the end of 1899, the last remnants of the Mahdist State had been destroyed. Sudan was not annexed to Egypt but was established as an Anglo-Egyptian condominium. From a legal point of view, sovereignty and administration were shared between Great Britain and Egypt, but in practice the Egyptians had a very limited influence over Sudan, which became part of the British colonial system in Africa.

Chapter 12

The American Campaigns of the British Army

The Patriot War, 1837–1840

When the USA gained its independence in 1783, Great Britain was able to retain possession of Canada, which remained the largest colony of the British Crown at a time when India was still administered by the private East India Company and Australia was only in the early phases of its colonization. From an administrative point of view, British Canada was divided into Lower Canada, Upper Canada, the Indian Department, Nova Scotia, New Brunswick, Newfoundland, Prince Edward Island and Cape Breton Island. The economies of all these territories had a particular role in the global commercial system created by Britain and were mostly based on the fur trade and fishing. Another important activity was the exploitation of forests for wood: during the long wars fought against Revolutionary and Napoleonic France, Canada was extremely important for Britain as a source of high-quality wood for the building of warships. Although Canada was not as economically developed as the USA, its population (albeit quite small) was made up of sturdy and courageous people. The province of Lower Canada corresponded to the former territory of New France and thus comprised most of the French-speaking settlers living in British North America. It had a much larger population than Upper Canada and comprised the three most important cities of British North America: Québec, Montréal and Trois-Rivières. The province of Upper Canada was mostly inhabited, at least initially, by loyalist Americans who abandoned the Thirteen Colonies during the American Revolution. Geographically, Upper Canada comprised the vast territory located between the western border of Québec province and the city of Windsor on Lake Huron. In 1815, the Indian Department of Canada was still mostly unsettled and was defended by just a few forts. Its only inhabitants were Francophone *voyageurs* (hunters) and fur traders. At the beginning of the nineteenth century, most of Canada's population consisted of Francophone settlers, so at the outbreak of the War of 1812 with the USA, the British authorities feared these men could refuse to serve in the militia or revolt against the Crown. Nevertheless, all the Canadian colonists remained loyal to Britain as they already considered their territories to be a nation and thus the foreign aggression of the USA did nothing but augment their patriotic feelings.

However, in November 1837, the Francophone population of Lower Canada rose up in revolt against the British under the guidance of the Parti Patriote, or Patriot Party, which for several years had been asking for political reforms that could augment the autonomy of the Canadian colonies and protect the rights of the Francophone community. This initial uprising did not involve large numbers of French-speaking Canadians and thus was suppressed quite easily by the British. The irregular forces assembled by the Patriots were defeated and their leaders were forced to flee to the USA as political exiles. Yet the British authorities soon realized that the Francophone rebels were merely reorganizing themselves in order to rise up again as soon as possible. Indeed, after establishing their bases south of the border, on US soil, the Patriots started gathering volunteers and weapons for a fresh insurrection. The British responded by deploying 5,000 soldiers in Lower Canada and creating a network of spies across the frontier with the USA. While these events took place in Lower Canada, the inhabitants of Upper Canada also rose up in revolt. The Anglophone settlers of the colony, like the Francophones of Lower Canada, asked the British government for a series of reforms favouring the autonomy of their homeland as well as the reorganization of their local economy now that the fur trade was no longer very lucrative. When the British failed to respond positively to the requests of the Canadians, the growing malcontent developed into an uprising. As had happened in Lower Canada, the initial revolt of Upper Canada was crushed quite rapidly and effectively by the British military, but it soon became apparent that a larger rebellion was about to break out and that the insurgents of Upper Canada were collaborating with the French-speaking ones.

In December 1837, the Canadian rebels established their base on Navy Island, a small inhabited island of the Ontario River on the border between Canadian Ontario and the US state of New York. The insurgents proclaimed the birth of a new state known as the Republic of Canada and continued their military operations against the British government by acting as pirates on Lake Erie and Lake Ontario. The Republican leaders hoped that the USA would support them, but this did not happen: the US authorities, in fact, collaborated with the British and intercepted any convoys of supplies heading for the Canadians. After suffering a series of military setbacks, the rebels changed strategy and restructured themselves as a secret organization known as the Frères Chasseurs, or Hunters' Lodge. They conducted a series of raids and incursions from their bases in the USA, causing the death of several people and significant material damage. In December 1838, the Canadian insurgents launched an invasion of Upper Canada, assembling a contingent of 400 men who marched on the city of Windsor. Here, however, they were utterly defeated by a British force that was supported by some US elements. The Battle of Windsor marked a turning point in what became known as the Patriot War, proving to the Canadian population that the use of force would have no positive results for its cause. By the beginning of 1839, the British government had despatched more than 10,000 regular soldiers to Canada in order to prevent the expansion of the rebellion. Consequently, soon after the Battle of Windsor, the Patriot War came to an end, both in Lower Canada and Upper Canada. However, the bloody events of 1837–38 convinced the British government that a series of reforms needed to be carried out in Canada in order to pacify the local population. What was known as 'Responsible Government' (i.e. political autonomy) was granted to the Canadian colonies, whose financial problems were progressively resolved by the British government with substantial investments (mostly involving the building of new infrastructure). A diversification of economic activities started to take place, together with an early form of industrialization. In 1840, through the Act of Union, Lower Canada and Upper Canada were merged as the single Province of Canada, which had its own autonomous Parliament.

The Fenian Raids and the Red River Rebellion, 1866–1870

No sooner had the American Civil War drawn to a close in 1865 than a new threat materialized south of the Canadian border in the guise of the Fenian Brotherhood, the American branch of the Irish Republican Army, which was formed in New York City in 1858. The Fenians were a strong military organization which wanted to achieve the independence of Ireland by invading a part of the British Empire, Canada. Most of its members were battle-hardened veterans of the American Civil War with extensive combat experience, who had been part of the Irish Brigade that fought for the Union Army. The Fenians attempted two invasions of Canadian territory, the first in 1866 and the second in 1870. These incursions were both repulsed by the Canadian Militia, which was supported by small numbers of British regulars. To operate against the Fenians, the Canadian and British forces were organized into temporary field brigades, each of which usually consisted of 1,000 Canadians and 500 British regulars plus fifty cavalrymen and 100 artillerymen. It is important to remember that, until 1870, a large portion of what is present-day northern Canada was not administered directly by the British government but by the Hudson's Bay Company, which exerted a monopoly over all the commercial activities connected with the fur trade that took place in the Arctic regions of Canada. The territories controlled by the Hudson's Bay Company consisted of three autonomous entities: Rupert's Land, North-Western Territory and British Columbia. Since 1850, the US government had started to exert an increasing pressure on the southern border of British Columbia, being keen to expand its territory at the expense of the Hudson's

Bay Company. The British government responded by establishing a permanent regular garrison in British Columbia (consisting of Royal Marines and Royal Engineers) and creating a new base for the Pacific Squadron of the Royal Navy at Esquimalt on Vancouver Island. On 19 November 1858, British Columbia ceased to be under the jurisdiction of the Hudson's Bay Company and became a new colony of the British Crown. Rupert's Land became part of Canada in 1868, followed by the North-Western Territory in 1870 and British Columbia in 1871.

The acquisition of such vast territories caused significant military issues to the Canadian government, since they had to be properly defended from both external and internal threats. The large northern lands that were annexed to Canada between 1868 and 1871 were mostly inhabited by native tribes and the Metis, individuals of mixed blood who – quite often – were Francophone. The Metis fur hunters and traders had been the backbone of the Hudson's Bay Company and had always lived quite similarly to the natives, with whom they had established very positive relations. The French-speaking fur hunters lived in a semi-nomadic way and were not used to recognizing the existence of any superior authority. As a result, when their homelands came under Canadian control, they initiated a long-lasting struggle for freedom. In 1870, the leader of the Metis, Louis Riel, established a provisional government in the northern territories with the objective of preserving their autonomy. Initially, the Canadian government tried to negotiate with the Metis, but when this became impossible a sizeable military force had to be sent against them in what became known as the Red River Expedition of 1870. Two battalions of Canadian militia marched against the rebels, together with seven companies of the King's Royal Rifle Corps and some detachments of the Royal Artillery and Royal Engineers. The expedition was a great success, ending the revolt without a single shot being fired; the Canadian troops – numbering some 1,400 men – swiftly traversed 1,200 miles of forested wilderness and without the loss of a single life. Riel fled to the USA as a political exile, while the Canadian authorities started organizing the new administration of the northern territories. From 1871, Canada was granted self-government and started to have a higher degree of political autonomy within the British Empire.

Chapter 13

The British Army in Australia and New Zealand

Australia

During the early nineteenth century, the interior regions of Australia became dangerous for the peaceful new colonists from Great Britain. These areas were inhabited by numerous Aboriginal groups as well as by the 'bushrangers', a term that referred to escaped convicts who preferred to risk the considerable hazards of life in the Australian wilderness than endure penal authority. Also known as 'absconders' or 'bolters', they lived in a savage way and perpetrated a series of crimes. Their living conditions were extremely harsh and they had very little by way of food resources, as a result of which the bushrangers embraced a life of banditry by preying on frontier farmers. The farmers were free settlers who had been encouraged to move to Australia and had been leased land by the British government. Such individuals, nicknamed 'squatters', were given convict labourers by the colonial authorities in order to develop their farms. For the colonial authorities, the only way to deal with the activities of the bushrangers and thus protect the squatters was to deploy mounted patrols that could operate in the bush. In 1825, a first detachment of mounted infantry (comprising twenty-five men) was formed within the 3rd Regiment of Foot that was part of Australia's garrison. Thanks to its excellent mobility, this first experimental corps operated with great success and intercepted a number of bushranger bands. This allowed a steady expansion into the open country located beyond Sydney Cove, which led to the creation of new colonial territories in addition to the original one of New South Wales. In 1825, the colony that later became known as Tasmania was established, being followed in 1829 by what was to be Western Australia. The colony of South Australia was formed in 1834, that of Victoria in 1851, Queensland in 1859 and Northern Territory in 1863. Gold was discovered in New South Wales and Victoria during 1851, which led to a massive gold rush that forever changed the nature of Australia. Between 1852 and 1860, many thousands of immigrants, mostly coming from Great Britain, travelled to Australia in search of gold. Soon becoming known as 'diggers', they started to build many new settlements, forging the identity of the modern Australian nation. The presence of so many newcomers and the discovery of large amounts of gold led to the birth of a new generation of bushrangers, who earned a living as bandits around the newly built boom towns of the diggers. Social tensions worsened, especially among the squatters and the new group of the 'selectors', newly arrived settlers who were given small land properties by the colonial government and were required to continue living upon them before they qualified for a permanent title. The daily life of the selectors was hard and impoverished, which brought the newcomers into conflict with the established and privileged squatters (who owned large ranches with massive herds of cattle and flocks of sheep). To protect the diggers from bandits and to prevent the outbreak of armed clashes between selectors and squatters, the colonial authorities had no option but to form new paramilitary police units to support the British regulars. In 1852, the 40th Regiment of Foot, which was stationed in Australia, was required to provide a mounted infantry detachment of 125 men to fight against the new generation of bushrangers. By 1871, however, Australia was granted self-government by Britain, thereby becoming much more of an independent nation.

New Zealand

The two major islands of New Zealand – South Island and North Island – were visited by the British maritime explorer James Cook in 1769. During the following years, they started attracting an increasing number of European whaling and sealing vessels, with the first serious contacts taking place between foreigners and the local Māori population. The warlike Māoris, quick to see the commercial advantages of trading with the whites, started exchanging flax for flintlock muskets. By the beginning of the nineteenth century, a number of small European coastal settlements had developed in New Zealand; these traded with the Māoris and served as ports of call for passing ships. These settlements were not controlled by any European colonial power, meaning their dealings with the Māoris were unregulated. They sold large numbers of modern firearms to the various Māori groups, which had enormous consequences for the natives' traditional society. Indeed, between 1820 and 1843, New Zealand was devastated by violent inter-tribal conflicts – fought with European weapons – that became known as the Musket Wars. At the beginning of the 1840s, the British – who by virtue of their Australian colonies considered New Zealand to be within their sphere of influence – decided to intervene in the Māori tribal politics in order to limit the growing influence that France and the USA were establishing over New Zealand. From 1844–46, the first major conflict – known as the Flagstaff War – was fought between Britain and the Māoris. This resulted in severe losses for the British, the warlike Māori fighting with enormous courage to preserve the independence of their homeland. Employing hit-and-run guerrilla tactics, the native warriors exploited the British Army's difficulties in operating in the wild and inhospitable terrain of New Zealand. Most of the Māoris were armed with modern weapons comparable to those used by the British and proved to be excellent marksmen. Each Māori tribe was also protected by strong fortifications. The outcome of the Flagstaff War was indecisive, and during the following decades the British continued fighting against the Māoris in order to establish their definitive control over New Zealand. These Māori Wars came to an end only in 1872, after the last resistance by the natives had been crushed.

Bibliography

Abbott, P., *Colonial Armies in Africa 1850–1918* (Foundry Books, 2009).
Barnes, R.M., *A History of the Regiments and Uniforms of the British Army* (Seeley Service, 1950).
Barthrop, M., *British Cavalry Uniforms Since 1660* (Blandford Press, 1984).
Barthorp, M., *British Infantry Uniforms Since 1660* (Blandford Press, 1982).
Barthorp, M., *The British Army on Campaign (1): 1816–1853* (Osprey Publishing, 1987).
Barthorp, M., *The British Army on Campaign (2): The Crimea 1854–1856* (Osprey Publishing, 1987).
Barthorp, M., *The British Army on Campaign (3): 1856–1881* (Osprey Publishing, 1988).
Barthorp, M., *The British Army on Campaign (4): 1882–1902* (Osprey Publishing, 1988).
Barthorp, M., *The British Troops in the Indian Mutiny 1857–1859* (Osprey Publishing, 1994).
Bayley, C.C., *Mercenaries for the Crimea: The German, Swiss and Italian Legions in British Service 1854–1856* (McGill-Queen's University Press, 1977).
Carman, W.Y., *Richard Simkin's Uniforms of the British Army: The Cavalry Regiments* (Webb & Bower, 1982).
Carman, W.Y., *Richard Simkin's Uniforms of the British Army: The Infantry Regiments* (Webb & Bower, 1985).
Chartrand, R., *British Forces in North America 1793–1815* (Osprey Publishing, 1998).
Chartrand, R., *Victoria's Canadian Militia* (Service Publications, 2016).
French, J., *The British in India 1826–1859* (Foundry Books, 2009).
Heath, I., *Armies of the 19th Century: China* (Foundry Books, 2009).
Heath, I., *The North-East Frontier 1837–1901* (Osprey Publishing, 1999).
Knight, I., *Boer Wars 1836–1898* (Osprey Publishing, 1996).
Knight, I., *Boer Wars 1898–1902* (Osprey Publishing, 1996).
Knight, I., *British Forces in Zululand 1879* (Osprey Publishing, 1991).
Lawson, Cecil C.P., *A History of the Uniforms of the British Army* (Littlehampton Book Services, 1974).
McBride, A., *The Zulu War* (Osprey Publishing, 1976).
Mollo, B., *The Indian Army* (Blandford Press, 1981).
Reid, S., *Queen Victoria's Highlanders* (Osprey Publishing, 2007).
Ross, D. & Tyler, G., *Canadian Campaigns 1860–1870* (Osprey Publishing, 1992).
Tylden, G., *The Armed Forces of South Africa 1659–1954* (Trophy Press, 1982).
Wilkinson-Latham, C., *North-West Frontier 1837–1947* (Osprey Publishing, 1977).
Wilkinson-Latham, C., *The Indian Mutiny* (Osprey Publishing, 1977).

Index

Assaye, 180

Basra, 188, 189

Canton, 195
Cawnpore, 194
Chernaya River, 177

Danubyu, 181
Dongola, 219

Gandamak, 190–1
Ghazni, 183–4
Golden Stool, 203, 207

Huron, Lake, 221

Jalalabad, 184

Keiskamma River, 200–202
Kharag, 187
Kumasi, 206–207

Lahore, 191, 193
Lucknow, 194

Majuba, 215
Malakoff Hill, 177

North Island, 226
Nsamankow, 204

Omdurman, 219, 220

Pra River, 205

Sand River, 213
Shalpuri Island, 180
South Island, 226
Sydney Cove, 225

Tana, Lake, 208

Ulundi, 214

Vaal River, 213

Yellow River, 196

Zula, 210–11

Dear Reader,

We hope you have enjoyed this book, but why not share your views on social media? You can also follow our pages to see more about our other products: facebook.com/penandswordbooks or follow us on X @penswordbooks

You can also view our products at www.pen-and-sword.co.uk (UK and ROW) or www.penandswordbooks.com (North America).

To keep up to date with our latest releases and online catalogues, please sign up to our newsletter at: www.pen-and-sword.co.uk/newsletter

If you would like a printed catalogue with our latest books, then please email: enquiries@pen-and-sword.co.uk or telephone: 01226 734555 (UK and ROW) or email: uspen-and-sword@casematepublishers.com or telephone: (610) 853-9131 (North America).

We respect your privacy and we will only use personal information to send you information about our products.

Thank you!